Say Yes to Life

Discover Your Pathways to
Happiness and Well-Being

Dr Linda Finnegan is a Principal Clinical Psychologist and Psychotherapist with many years' experience of helping people to overcome obstacles and find meaning and joy in their lives. She has trained in Clinical Psychology, Cognitive Behavioural Therapy, Humanistic and Integrative Psychotherapy and Body Psychotherapy.

Christy Kenneally is a bestselling novelist, poet, broadcaster and communications consultant. He is well known internationally for his work in the area of bereavement and loss. He lectures and runs workshops for voluntary and corporate groups on the areas of resilience, change, conflict, communication and teamwork and is an acclaimed after-dinner speaker.

For information about forthcoming publications, talks and workshops visit
www.discoveringpathways.com
or
email Christy at christykenn@eircom.net

Christy Kenneally is also the author of five novels, including *Second Son*, *The Remnant*, *Tears of God*, *The Betrayed* and *Sons of Cain*. He has also written a book on bereavement called *Life After Loss*.

Say Yes to Life

Discover Your Pathways to
Happiness and Well-Being

DR LINDA FINNEGAN

CHRISTY KENNEALLY

HACHETTE
BOOKS
IRELAND

First published in Ireland in 2013 by Hachette Books Ireland
First published in paperback in 2014 by Hachette Books Ireland
A division of Hachette UK Ltd.

1

The recommendations given in this book are solely intended as education
and information.

A CIP catalogue record for this title is available from the British Library

ISBN 978 1444 743609

Layout design and typeset by redrattledesign.com

Printed and bound by Clays Ltd, St Ives plc

Hachette Books Ireland policy is to use papers that are natural, renewable and
recyclable products and made from wood grown in sustainable forests. The logging and
manufacturing processes are expected to conform to the environmental regulations
of the country of origin.

Hachette Books Ireland
8 Castlecourt Centre
Castleknock
Dublin 15

A division of Hachette UK Ltd
338 Euston Rd
London
NW1 3 BH

www.hachette.ie

For Shane and Stephen

Acknowledgements

It would not have been possible to complete this book without the support of a number of people. We would especially like to thank Ciara Doorley and Claire Rourke (Editor), for their hard work, encouragement and support. We would also like to thank Breda Purdue and Jim Binchy of Hachette Ireland, and our literary agent Jonathan Williams.

A number of people read the manuscript and gave us very valuable feedback. In particular we would like to thank Lorraine Grennan, Mairin Begley, Barbara Fitzgerald, Michael Byrne and Professor Alan Carr.

The Somatic and Meditative practices in this book are influenced by the work of Barbara Fitzgerald, Psychotherapist and by Linda's training in body psychotherapy with David and Silvia Boadella at the International Institute for Biosynthesis, Heiden, Switzerland.

Special thanks to colleagues at the Department of Psychology & Psychotherapy, and all the staff of the HSE Adult Mental Health Services at St James's Hospital, Dublin for their ongoing support.

We would also like to thank the many people we have been privileged to work with who have shared their pain and joy and taught us how important it is to say yes to life.

Very special love and thanks to our sons Shane and Stephen, who bore the burden of co-authoring parents with their usual grace and keep us grounded with their humour and enthusiasm.

Contents

The Pathways

Poems by Christy Kenneally

Before You Set Out

'There must be more to life.' How often have you said this? Whether you spoke in exasperation or hope, you were really saying that you wished your life could be better. It may be that you feel stuck or unhappy in your life right now but are unsure about how to move forward. Or maybe you have already begun to make changes and need some support. Whatever the reason, something has drawn you to our particular book and prompted you to open the cover and begin to read. Was it the title? The invitation to 'say yes to life'. Was it the subtitle and the possibility of discovering pathways that will lead you to a happier and fuller life?

Can you allow yourself to be curious about what within you is trying to emerge and needs encouragement?

Say Yes to Life contains a positive, hopeful invitation, but we know it can be hard to be hopeful when you have lost a loved one or your job's on the line and you're struggling to make ends meet. At these times in our lives, we can reach the depths of our own despair, when our 'no' can seem stronger and more powerful than our 'yes'. But during these emotional winters are things really as hopeless as they seem? What if you had a treasure chest of resources that you had built up over time, but had stashed away and forgotten? Imagine what it would be like for you to access these resources and find a way to reconnect with your own power, hope, strength, joy, creativity, humour and imagination.

Say Yes to Life is about using this rich store of abilities and resources – which you hold inside yourself – to turn your life around. It is a step-by-step guide to unlocking your potential, so that you can lead a fuller and happier life. We will help you use your own ability to endure, adapt and transform, and we will also show you how to acknowledge, accept and learn to live with your own vulnerability.

At times, we will invite you to reflect and to become more aware of how you feel, think and behave, and we have created space in the book for you to record these reflections as part of your journey. In this way, we will help you to build and nurture your inner strengths and resources and show you how to reignite your vitality and reconnection with the life that is within and around you.

The therapeutic approaches we use in this book draw on the rich clinical traditions and expertise of cognitive behavioural therapy, body psychotherapy, mindfulness, and integrative and humanistic psychotherapy.

In the past, psychologists have approached change and growth by focusing on human problems and deficits. However, there is now a focus on building human strengths and nurturing positive emotions to enhance personal happiness and well-being. In his book, *Positive Psychology: The Science of Happiness and Human Strengths*,[1] Professor Alan Carr has provided an extensive review of the research in this area. We know from this research that unresolved loss, destructive anger, perfectionism, unrealistic expectations, negative self-talk, worry and distorted thinking patterns can block our path to a happy and fulfilled life.

In this book, each of these blocks to happiness is explored, enabling us to guide you through the different ways of dealing with and overcoming the challenges they present. As well as overcoming these blocks to happiness, we will also help you to build positive emotional experiences, which is another important step on the path to a happier and more fulfilled life. A number of pathways in this book – like 'Dare to Dream', 'Be Thankful', 'Let Laughter In', 'Connect with Your Community', 'Nourish Your Relationships', 'Rediscover Nature' and 'Allow Your Soul to Sing' – will help you build positive emotional experiences.

Each of the twenty pathways you will explore in this book rests on a firm foundation of psychological research and clinical practice. The chapters build on each other and are designed to be worked through in the sequence in which they are presented. However, you may feel drawn to a particular chapter, and want to read it first – this is understandable if there is a particular issue you want to address, but we would encourage you to then work through the other chapters in sequence. We also suggest that you keep a journal to record your thoughts and feelings as you work through the exercises and reflective practices.

Say Yes to Life contains reflections, poems and stories from our lives to raise, stretch and soothe your spirit as you make the journey to a more fulfilled and happier you.

As a couple, we have known each other for thirty-five years, and we celebrated our thirtieth wedding anniversary while writing this book. Working together on *Say Yes to Life* has been a thoughtful, exciting, emotional journey that has helped us to reconnect with and say yes to what we value most in life.

Because we have both contributed to the book, it may not always be clear which one of us is 'speaking', but we feel that the message is more important than who is speaking at any given time. All the poems in the book have been written by Christy.

We couldn't have written *Say Yes to Life* without having experienced periods in our own lives when hope seemed in short supply. At these times, we were lucky enough to rediscover our own personal and combined strengths, which enabled us to move on to a better quality of life. Certainly, we got help and support from many along the way, but the challenge of finding, freeing and engaging with our own potential remains an ongoing journey for both of us.

Professionally, we have a combined half century of working with people who have experienced loss, heartbreak and crippling self-doubt. In this book, whenever we refer to other people, we have changed their names and personal details to protect their privacy. Our own experiences, and the life experiences others have shared with us, have convinced us that if we can all tap into and connect with the power of our own resilience, we can survive. In fact, we can do better than survive – we can transform our lives.

We look forward to travelling with you as you explore the different pathways to happiness and well-being in our book, and we wish you well on your journey.

Linda and Christy

www.discoveringpathways.com
Email: christykenn@eircom.net

Pathway One

Recognise Your Resilience

When I was growing up, it never rained in Cork, but a lot of rain blew in from Kerry.

'Rain, beginning in the west, will spread eastwards,' the forecasters on the radio said.

'They make it over there,' someone sighed.

Rain or fine, I went to meet my dad at half-past five. He would always have a story about a Kite he'd seen hovering over the southside, or an Arctic tern swooping for bread behind the factory. Once, he claimed an owl had stared him down from the lintel of Creedon's Bakery.

I would stand on a step where the rivers of five roads collided and pooled before the cathedral. Domed with a fisherman's hat and tented in a plastic Mac, I'd watch the workers come home through the rain. Most of the men walked fast, as if they could outpace the drops. The women grimaced under umbrellas, averting their eyes from the rude, battering downpour. Everyone looked down, hunched beneath the burden of a bad day.

My dad rounded the corner at Walsh's Pharmacy with a steady step. He held his head high and swung his arms as if he was walking Nash's boreen on a summer's day. He fielded my jump as he passed the steps and hoisted me up in his arms. I remember drops of water in his hair and a big drop swinging from his earlobe like a pirate's earring. I asked him why – why did he hold his head high on such an awful day? He had every reason to bend, having shouldered my mother to her grave a year earlier. He hitched me higher and tapped my chin with his wet fist.

'Never drop your head, boy,' he said. 'Good day or bad, never look down.'

At certain times in our lives we can reach the depths of our own despair. During these emotional winters, our future can appear bleak and our hope larder can seem terribly bare. But is it really bare? What if you had a treasure chest of resources and abilities that you had built up over time, stashed away and forgotten? What would it be like if, at these times, you were able to find a way to connect with your own power, strength, creativity, humour and imagination? Discovering the power of your own resilience will enable you to make this connection.

Resilience is the human capacity to endure, to overcome, adapt and be transformed by life's adversities. It is that tremendous ability to bounce back. A resilient person is like a tree rooted in nourishing soil that stays supple and sways before strong winds while its dry and brittle companions crack and crash to the forest floor. It is the muscle we develop in tough times that enables us to bend and not break, and in that process to become stronger. Resilience is about being flexible, but not hardened.

In olden times, swords would often shatter in battle. Then the swordsmiths of Toledo in Spain became famous for the flexibility of their swords. Their secret was to transfer the blades back and forth from extreme heat to extreme cold until the metal was properly tempered. The test for a tempered blade was for someone to bend the tip to touch the hilt. A Toledo blade would bend but not break.

As human beings, we demonstrate time after time that we *can* cope with extraordinary circumstances. After tsunamis, tornados, eruptions or earthquakes have rearranged landscapes and wiped away people and homes, those left behind somehow find the strength and motivation to rebuild. People who suffer horrific experiences of abuse, torture or trauma have the capacity to work through and integrate these experiences and to go on to live meaningful and fulfilling lives.

The human capacity of resilience transforms and deepens our lives and spirits. Resilient people don't ignore the pain and disappointment of failure or loss, but they don't remain identified with it either – it doesn't define who they are. When disaster happens, resilient people look back and question what they can learn about themselves and about life. What could I have done better in terms of preparation or performance? What was outside of my control? What supports would have helped me? They go on to put that learning into practice so that every challenge, win or lose, is a step in the learning process, helping them build up the muscle of resilience. Resilience is like a muscle that you have been building from the time you were born. When you learn to tap into the power and strength of your own resilience, you will never lose hope.

How resilient do you think you are?

Take a minute to consider this question and rate yourself on a scale of 0–10, with 0 being not at all resilient and 10 being extremely resilient.

On a scale of 0–10, I would give myself a score of _____
We will return to this question at the end of this chapter.

Characteristics of resilient people

Let's consider some of the characteristics of resilient people. Think of a character from a movie, book or television show you find inspiring and whom you consider to be resilient.

In the space below, name the character and say why you have chosen them.

_____

_____

_____

Describe any challenges that this character had to overcome.

_____

_____

_____

Identify the qualities and abilities that this character demonstrated that made you identify them as being resilient.

_____

_____

_____

Is there anyone you know in your own life that you would describe as resilient? It could be a family member, parent, grandparent, colleague or neighbour. Describe some of the challenges they have had to overcome in their life.

_____

_____

_____

Describe some of the qualities you think the person you have chosen possessed which helped them to deal with – and which were strengthened by dealing with – the challenges that life presented.

_____

_____

_____

_____

From the moment we are born, we are faced with challenges – to have our cry heard, to take our first steps and to begin again when we fall over. As we grow older, more challenges present themselves. The challenge of leaving home, the break-up of a relationship, the experience of betrayal in friendship or love, and the challenge of coping with death or trauma.

Take a moment to consider your own life to date and describe some of the mental, physical and psychological challenges and adversities that you have had to face and overcome from when you were very small to the present day. Try to identify at least two from each decade of your life.

_____

_____

_____

_____

_____

_____

_____

From the list of experiences you have identified, pick the three that you think have challenged you most. Were you able to access any supports and resources to help you overcome these experiences and move on in your life?

_____

_____

_____

_____

_____

_____

_____

For the three most challenging experiences you have identified, name some of the core qualities and strengths you have that helped you overcome the experience and move on in your life.

_____

_____

_____

_____

_____

_____

_____

_____

_____

The building blocks of resilience

Becoming more aware of the different building blocks or features of your resilience will enable you to activate that resilience and step into your own power.

The building blocks of resilience fall into three main categories:

- external supports and resources

- social and interpersonal skills

- personal qualities and strengths.

External supports and resources

We all need the help and support of others at different times in our lives. These supports come in many shapes and forms and have been built up by us through our network of relationships, friendships and involvements within our communities.

What are the range of external supports and resources that are available to you in your life? External resources can also include community supports, membership of sporting clubs or organisations, pets or your home or garden or local environment.

To help you identify them, compose six sentences that begin with 'I have'. For example, 'I have friends who care about me', 'I have a supportive partner', 'I have a supportive family.'

I have _____

I have _____

I have _____

I have _____

I have _____

I have _____

When you have completed this list, take a moment to read each sentence aloud. Describe how you feel when you acknowledge these supports.

_____

_____

_____

_____

Are there any ways in which you can use these external supports and resources more to help you in your life right now?

_____

_____

_____

_____

_____

_____

Are there any external supports or resources that you think you could begin to develop and include in your life?

_____

_____

_____

Social and interpersonal skills

An important aspect of our resilience is the range of social and interpersonal skills we possess. We often take these for granted but they are very important tools that we use to help us overcome difficulties in our lives.

What are the different social and interpersonal skills you have that are part of your resilience?

To help you identify them, compose six sentences that begin with 'I can'. For example, 'I can plan well', 'I can listen well', 'I can ask for help when I need it', 'I can problem solve.' It may help to think of a recent problem that you feel you have dealt with successfully.

I can _____

I can _____

I can _____

I can _____

I can _____

I can _____

When you have completed your list, take a moment to read each sentence aloud. Did anything surprise you? Describe how you feel when you acknowledge these skills.

_____

_____

_____

_____

Are there any ways you can use these skills more in your life right now?

_____

_____

_____

_____

Are there any skills that you would like to develop?

_____

_____

_____

_____

What supports do you need to develop these skills?

_____

_____

_____

_____

Personal qualities and strengths

Feeling down or depressed is a bit like wearing sunglasses indoors on a winter's day – everything appears even more bleak and gloomy. It becomes almost impossible to see any chinks of light and this, in turn, fuels a negative view of the world and of ourselves, making things seem even more gloomy. The heaviness of this dark blanket can be very disempowering. We feel like there is nothing we can do to change things, dismay sets in and, at these times, we lose sight of our own strengths and potential. When you learn to identify your core strengths and begin to reuse these strengths in your daily life, your sense of well-being and your relationship with yourself and others will begin to change significantly.

Key points about our strengths:
- We all have many core strengths.
- These strengths can be a very valuable resource to help us rebuild our sense of well-being.
- We can all lose sight of these inner resources and aspects of who we are, particularly at times when we feel down or overwhelmed.
- We can reopen our connections to these inner resources. This reconnection can be very empowering.

Complete the following exercises and reflections to help you reconnect with the important aspects of your essential self.

Take a moment to read the following list of forty core strengths and circle six that you believe you have, even if you don't feel connected with that quality at the moment.

Generous : Brave : Humorous : Warm :
Open-minded : Joyful : Fair : Honest :

Curious : Giving : Caring : Loyal : Self-control:
Compassionate : Committed : Idealistic :
Playful : Kind : Sociable : Thoughtful : Spiritual:
Leadership : Trustworthy : Loving : Assertive :
Creative : Passionate : Forgiving : Considerate :
Grateful : Modest : Competent : Persevering :
Hopeful : Resilient : Genuine : Dedicated :
Authentic : Reliable : Wisdom

Next, write down these six core strengths, starting with 'I am' or 'I have':

I _____

I _____

I _____

I _____

I _____

I _____

When you have identified your top six core strengths, read them aloud and make a note of any feelings you have at the end of this exercise.

_____

_____

_____

If possible, also ask someone you trust and are close to to read this list and identify the core strengths that they feel apply to you.

Compare the two lists. Has your trusted person identified a quality in you that you have overlooked? Did anything surprise you about the qualities they see in you?

_____

_____

_____

_____

For each of the qualities you have listed, try to describe an example of how you express this in your life. For example, if you have said 'I am playful', you might say that you know this about yourself because: 'When my nieces and nephews come round, I really love to have fun with them.'

1. I am _____

I know this about myself because _____

_____

_____

_____

2. I am _____

I know this about myself because _____

_____

_____

_____

3. I am _____

I know this about myself because _____

_____

_____

_____

4. I am _____

I know this about myself because _____

_____

_____

_____

5. I am _____

I know this about myself because _____

_____

_____

_____

6. I am _____

I know this about myself because _____

_____

_____

_____

Now, take a moment and read aloud the answers you have written.

Take your time with this and speak slowly. It may seem a bit strange, but it is really important that you allow yourself to receive and hear this feedback to yourself. If there are people around and you don't feel you can do this right now, do it later or go to a place where you can be alone.

When you have read the statements out loud once, pause and say them aloud again, but this time say them slowly and listen to yourself as you speak.

Make a note of how it felt to do this exercise.

_____

_____

_____

Give an example of a time in your life when you used one of your core strengths and it made a significant difference not only to others but also to how you felt in yourself.

_____

_____

_____

_____

Describe in detail what happened and what your core strength enabled you to do.

_____

_____

_____

_____

_____

_____

_____

Take some time to remember what it felt like to use this core strength and what feelings you were left with afterwards. Recall any emotions or memories that come to mind.

I felt _____

_____

_____

_____

Sometimes, we reserve our core strengths for other people and have very little left over for ourselves. What would it be like if you could be 'generous' or 'kind' or 'playful' or 'loving' towards yourself? Imagine what that might feel like.

Ask yourself the following question:

If you could feel more connected to your top three core strengths of _____, _____ and _____, how might this make a difference in the way that you relate to and judge yourself?

In thinking about your answer, try to imagine yourself actively engaging each of the particular strengths you have identified.

_____

_____

_____

_____

_____

_____

Each evening in your journal make a note of any core strength you used during the day, no matter how small or to what degree. Write about the situation and how you felt afterwards. Then, take a moment to brainstorm ways of extending the use of your core strengths in your daily life.

Earlier in the chapter we asked you to rate yourself in terms of resilience on a scale of 0–10. Having worked through the exercises, take a moment to rate yourself again and compare the two scores. Are the scores the same or have they changed? Make a note of any difference below.

_____

_____

_____

Name one or two key points that struck a chord with you about your own resilience when you were completing the exercises in this chapter.

_____

_____

_____

Take a moment to reflect on how this might make a difference to you in your life in terms of how you feel about yourself, how you think or how you might behave in the future.

_____

_____

_____

_____

_____

_____

You have known hard times,
Known heartache and sorrow
But you're still here.
All you have learned from life
Does not just disappear.
New strength is gained and stored
Through every tear.
When future trials seem many
And resources few
Call up your hard-won courage
And believe in you.

Even if you don't feel particularly resilient at the moment, there are many ways in which you can continue to build and strengthen your resilience. These include looking at how you interpret and give meaning to what happens to you, learning to talk back to your own negativity, broadening and developing your relationships and social supports, setting realistic goals, and fostering positive emotional experiences in your life. In the chapters that follow, we will outline ways that will help you to do this.

Pathway Two

Reach Beyond

Bird in a cage
Why flutter to and fro?
This small sky is all you know.
What need have you for flight?
Hawk stoops, crows rage,
Be safe within your wing-span cage.
And yet,
When, by the window, wild birds fly,
You lift your wings to soar
And so do I.

Borders are often patrolled, mined or walled. In some cases, it is to keep foreigners out – in others, it is how rulers contain their own people.

Closed borders magnify difference. Those on the other side from where we stand grow grotesque and threatening if we are deprived of their contact. Those on the inside become insulated against the reality of the rest of the world.

The ancient maps bore a legend scribbled across the border: 'Beyond this point,' they claimed, 'be demons, dragons, sirens and whirlpools.'

These words served as a warning that proclaimed it was better to stay in your own place, among your own people, than risk finding yourself in such a place. It was best to follow in your father's footsteps, to dream small, local dreams and to aspire no higher than everyone else.

Children would accept these boundaries and tailor their dreams to fit the received wisdom and the aspirations of being 'smaller' people.

It is tempting to live in the Comfort Zone. The Comfort Zone borders the lands of possibility and potential. The inhabitants of the Comfort Zone describe themselves as normal, sensible and prudent. Their motto is: 'There's no place like here.' Their national flower is a geranium in a clay pot. Any talk of elsewhere is regarded as treasonous, a slur on the perfection of here. Children are taught never to dream, yearn or hope for anything because everything is here. Elsewhere is foreign, dangerous and inferior. 'Lower your sail,' they are told; 'only a fool would sail to the rim of the horizon. Paddle in the shallows,' they are advised; 'deep water may drown you. Don't gaze at the stars, you'll most likely trip over a stone.'

But the inhabitants of the Comfort Zone are not evil people – they are just scared people. They would like us to play by the rules and be content 'for our own good'.

Someone wrote the story of the Comfort Zone long ago and the story remains unchanged. It is the story of how things were, are and should always be. Questioning the story is suspect, adding to the story is forbidden.

Everything in the Comfort Zone is here today and here again tomorrow.

What we know becomes the boundary of our knowing. What we accept becomes the limit of our loving. What we see with our own eyes can blind us to other visions.

In ancient times, the horizon was somewhere sailors didn't sail. They perceived the world as flat – who would want to sail over the edge? They made sure they kept land in sight at all times. The great explorers became great because they dared to sail over the rim of the horizon. The great thinkers thought to look beyond the limits of their own knowing.

Any aspiration needs the oxygen of encouragement. However, sometimes that oxygen is cut off by others. A child may want to be a scientist, an opera singer, an astronaut or a professional footballer, and the temptation for those who love them is to 'lower the bar'. Phrases like 'only a very small number of people get to be astronauts' or 'for every professional footballer there are a thousand who never made the grade' trip from the tongues of the well-meaning.

It can take years to recover from the crushing effect of having a ditch flung on your dreams.

Why not affirm the dream? Why not encourage children to study hard or practise their football skills, or throw themselves into the study of physics or the joy of playing in the kids' leagues? In other words, why not encourage them to live their dream now?

'Now' is such a vital word. If we could only move our focus to 'now' without demolishing the possibility of 'then'.

Does encouraging children in this way mean they will realise their dream? Maybe – or maybe their dreams will change. It is not about the final destination; rather it is about the journey. Our dreams can change, expand and move in different directions as we grow in relationship with ourselves.

Take a moment to recall some of the hopes and dreams you had when you were younger.

_____

_____

_____

_____

_____

Were there any ways in which your dreams were discouraged or not supported?

_____

_____

_____

_____

_____

What impact did this lack of support or encouragement have on you at the time?

_____

_____

_____

_____

_____

Describe any ways in which you were encouraged and supported to achieve your dreams.

_____

_____

_____

_____

_____

Who has encouraged you most in your life and what difference has this made to you?

_____

_____

_____

_____

If you were to speak words of encouragement to yourself, what would you say?

_____

_____

_____

_____

Allow yourself to name some dreams that you have for yourself and your life right now. When you do this, try not to limit your dreams in any way. Do this exercise even if you are not sure how to achieve the dreams you mention.

_____

_____

_____

_____

_____

Making the impossible possible

The word 'impossible' is a conversation stopper. It is also a dream-buster, censoring the dream and excluding the dreamer from the higher reaches of possibility.

Do you remember being called a 'dreamer' at home or in school? It wasn't exactly a compliment, was it? And yet, many of the wonderful inventions we take for granted were 'dreamed' by people who thought outside the limits of possibility. The fact is that the human spirit laughs in the face of impossibility, as human history proves. The impossible for one generation is the discovery of the next and part of the ordinary and everyday for the generation after that.

Our great-grandparents looked up at the moon and accepted the impossibility of ever looking back from there. To another generation, the earth was flat and at the centre of the universe. To us, the earth is the tiniest speck in a small galaxy in an ever-expanding universe.

We have flown to and beyond the upper reaches and dived to the deepest depths. We have tamed diseases that decimated previous generations and have grafted new sight and hearts. The list of what was impossible but is now taken for granted is endless. In the light of this litany of discovery, who would venture to say that anything is impossible?

In many ways, the last frontier of what is possible is within ourselves. Despite being surrounded by proofs to the contrary, we can still adopt a stance of 'personal impossibility' and limit our horizons in terms of personal growth and achievement.

Dissatisfaction with the way things are now is the motivation to reach beyond ourselves to new possibilities. But when we are confronted with that challenge, a challenge that comes from deep inside ourselves, our first response is frequently to be overwhelmed by the 'how'. That question focuses us on the mechanics of change, and often we measure our resources against the task and come up short. We may still attempt the change but our sense of inadequacy sucks energy from our effort and we fail. That failure can confirm our belief that it was never possible in the first place.

The crucial question to ask is not about 'how' but 'why'. If we know the 'why', the 'how' will emerge.

When our younger son was even younger, I collected him from school and asked him if he liked his teacher.

'Yes,' he said, 'she is a great teacher.'

'What makes her such a great teacher?' I prompted.

'She thinks sideways,' he said.

The great innovators, inventors and problem solvers thought sideways.

The engineer John Savage, who masterminded the Hoover Dam, experienced a huge setback. The design of the retaining wall of the dam would work perfectly if they could fix the ends to the canyon walls. Every time they tried, the canyon walls crumbled. But John stuck to the task, shifted his thinking sideways from the norm and brought in huge refrigeration units to freeze the canyon walls until the concrete set.

Are there any ways in which you hold yourself back or set limits for yourself that serve to keep you restricted in your life? It may be something that you are doing or not doing, or it may be ways in which you criticise or judge yourself.

I hold myself back when I _____

_____

_____

_____

Take a moment to imagine the possibilities that might open up for you if you no longer held yourself back.

If I didn't hold myself back I might _____

_____

_____

_____

Identify three steps you can take to begin to open up more possibilities for you in your life. You might decide to stop *doing something that is holding you back or you may consider* starting *something that would enable you to expand more in your life.*

_____

_____

_____

_____

Masks we wear

Among the prized possessions in our home is our collection of masks from around the world. The wearing of masks is a practice common to many different cultures. In ancient times, people put on masks for rituals and the masks represented the gods or demons they would have to appease or the most fearsome aspects of themselves so they could intimidate their enemies. In our time, they are mostly fun objects, things we don for Halloween, for the purpose of mutual scaring and connecting with our playful side.

In every time, masks have been used to hide the face, identity and personality, and perhaps vulnerability, of the wearer.

Sometimes the mask we wear can hold us back.

We learn from childhood to wear masks, to put on a face appropriate to a role or situation. For example, a young man and woman want to appear at their best when they meet, and so they prepare their masks. He presses a clean shirt (front only); she creates a new hole in the ozone layer with a spray of perfume. Both want to project the best versions of themselves so the best version of him meets the best version of her. It is only after a hundred – small – revelations of likes, dislikes, opinions and hopes that they take off that perfect mask and reveal their real selves. That revelation is the true starting point of a real relationship.

There are a number of reasons why we wear masks. Sometimes it's because we have been taught through experience that it is best to be cautious when we encounter another and that we should be slow to reveal ourselves. We learn to pull down visors to protect us while our confidence and trust develop. Masking is part of our preliminary protection as we discover the personality, character and intentions of the other person. As the 'identikit picture' of the other forms in our minds, we decide whether or not to reveal different aspects of ourselves which will enable us to engage at a deeper level with the other person. It takes us time to gauge whether this person is trustworthy; worthy of being entrusted with our 'real' selves.

Occasionally, it happens spontaneously. A bus journey in the company of a stranger can begin with small talk about the weather. It can progress from that, with exhilarating rapidity, to the big things in our lives. And the road flies by and the terminus comes too soon. Maybe it's because we establish that neither of us is an axe-murderer and that we're strangers to each other and unlikely to meet again. With that kind of anonymity, who needs a mask? But it is a special encounter and all the more precious for being so rare.

Sometimes we learn to wear masks because of experiences of breach of trust or betrayal. In our wounding, we retreat behind our mask and vow never to allow ourselves be that vulnerable again.

We also learn to wear a mask when the role we feel we must play assumes more importance than the needs of our true self. We become locked in to relating as mother, son, teacher, granny. We can fall in love with and over-identify with a particular role because it is familiar and gives us a sense of fulfilment and satisfaction.

It can be hard to move between roles.

A policeman told me how his nine-year-old was suspected of keeping some money that didn't belong to him. He sat him on a kitchen chair and began to interrogate him.

'I walked up and down behind him,' he said, 'just like I'd do at the station; asking him questions and catching inconsistencies in his story. And suddenly, I was struck by the awfulness of what I was doing. I was interrogating my child as a policeman and not talking to him as his dad.'

There is no point in hanging up the uniform at the end of the day but staying in the role.

Clergy and medics often get trapped in their roles when tragedy strikes their own loved ones. They can be expected to respond to their family's needs rather than experience their own needs as members of the family. Clergy in particular are expected to perform their official duties for their deceased parent and comfort their siblings. It is unfortunate when someone is appreciated and admired for their role while their real selves can wither away from lack of love.

Role transitions are often painful and pose questions about our identity that we can find difficult to answer. Who am I if I am no longer in the role of mother, son, daughter, father? The parent may be tempted to remain as the parent and 'mother' the grown child as if they were still small and dependent. And the child might find it equally difficult to grow up and away from the child role. Ideally roles change, evolve, and relationships adapt and grow with that change.

The most important thing about putting on a mask is knowing when to take it off. Modern masks don't placate gods or demons or intimidate enemies, but they can limit the vision, potential and quality of life of those who wear them. We can become trapped behind our masks and, while initially they may have offered protection, they eventually limit us and block us from reaching our full potential.

The following exercises will help you explore your relationship with the different roles you have in your life and the masks you wear.

Describe the different roles that you have in your life. For example, mother, daughter, son, grandparent, work role, wife, lover, friend or student.

_____

_____

_____

Now write a sentence to describe how you see yourself in each of these roles.

_____

_____

_____

_____

_____

_____

Are there any masks you wear in these roles?

_____

_____

_____

_____

_____

_____

For each of your roles describe what it is your masks are trying to conceal.

_____

_____

_____

_____

_____

_____

In what ways have your masks helped you in your life?

_____

_____

_____

_____

_____

In what ways are the masks you wear holding you back? What quality in you is trying to emerge from behind the mask?

_____

_____

_____

_____

_____

_____

_____

_____

How can you encourage and support what is trying to emerge in you?

_____

_____

_____

_____

_____

_____

There are no limits.
Each passing day
Reveals another way.
The circle that we know
Is but one ripple
In the outward flow
Of wonders yet to see.

There are no limits.
Each passing year
Removes another fear.
The person I am now
Must wrestle with the why,
And what and how
And who I yet may be.

There are no limits.
The buds let go
To flex, unfurl and grow.
The person I will be
Is reaching far beyond
The here and now
And yearning to be free.

Pathway Three

Challenge Your Thinking

A famous soccer manager once said:

'Some people believe football is a matter of life and death. I am very disappointed with that attitude. I can assure you it is much, much more important than that.'

As a boy, I took sport very seriously but I was deadly serious about winning. Winning was what it was all about. After all, who wanted to be a loser? For me, it was all or nothing. If you won, you were on top of the world; if you lost, you were nothing. My grandfather had a different view.

I remember once, after a football final, walking into his house and slinging my football boots in the corner.

'Did you win or lose?' he asked.

'We were beaten,' I said dejectedly.

'No!' he said emphatically. 'We can win or lose but we are never beaten.'

In sport, winning or losing are separated by a hair's breadth. A deflection, an injury, everything from an 'off day' to the weather can mean laurels or lamentations. Negative interpretations and thoughts are demoralising. They can give rise to feelings of dejection, disappointment and shame. They lead us to consider 'packing it in', or 'accepting the inevitable'. We carry that mindset to the next encounter, convinced that we haven't a chance, and this then becomes a self-fulfilling prophecy.

Our perception and interpretation of an event can have a huge impact on how we think and feel about ourselves, others and the world around us. For that reason, it is really important that we give some time to thinking about thinking – in particular to thinking about our own style and way of thinking.

It may surprise you, but your pattern of thinking may be playing a key role in keeping you stuck emotionally. You might say, 'My thoughts are my thoughts. I can't do anything about them, so what's the point?'

Well, the point is that you *can* do something. Not only can you change the way you think but, as a result, you can also change how you feel and how you behave.

Thinking about thinking

In this chapter, and the one that follows, 'Talk Back to Negative Self-Talk', we will introduce you to ways of becoming more aware of your thinking style and we will show you not only how to identify thinking errors or biases that may have crept into your mindset over time, but also how to challenge and change these negative thinking patterns to enable you to feel better within yourself and relate more positively to those around you.

Firstly, there are two core principles that are important to take on board:

1. we feel what we feel because of the *way* that we think
2. thoughts are *just* thoughts – they are *not* facts.

The way we think

One of the important contributions of cognitive behavioural therapy (CBT) is the way in which it highlights the relationship between how we feel and what we think. In fact, cognitive behavioural therapists would say that we feel what we feel because of the *way* we think, and that our way of thinking is not cast in stone – it needs to be reviewed and challenged, particularly when it is keeping us stuck in negative emotional states.

In many cases, it is not what happens to us that affects how we feel, and subsequently how we behave, but our interpretation of what happens, the meaning we attribute to it.

Over four hundred years ago, Shakespeare got there first when he wrote in *Hamlet* that nothing is either good or bad but thinking makes it so.[2]

How does this relationship between our thoughts and our feelings work?

Let's take an example.

You go into the staff canteen at lunch-time and sit down at a table where other staff members are talking animatedly about the previous night's soccer game.

You sit there for a few minutes; nobody talks to you.

You begin to think, *They're ignoring me. They must find me very boring. They probably didn't want me to sit down here in the first place.*

These thoughts lead to a rush of feelings, including sadness, disappointment and anger. As these feelings develop, you become aware of them in your body. You become aware that your heart is pounding and your hands are sweating.

You then think, *People will notice I am upset and I will look stupid.*

These new thoughts add a second layer of emotions. As well as feeling sadness, disappointment and anger, you now feel embarrassed and humiliated. You react by keeping your head down, hoping no one will notice. You gulp your lunch down quickly and leave the table as soon as possible. As you leave the canteen, you vow not to go there again and to eat your lunch at your desk instead.

Remember, we feel what we feel because of the way that we think and this influences how we behave.

Now, once more, imagine the same scenario.

You go into the staff canteen at lunch-time and sit down at a table where other staff members are talking animatedly about the previous night's soccer game.

You sit there for a few minutes; nobody talks to you.

This time your thoughts are, *Gosh, these guys are so passionate about that game that they don't even notice I am here. It must have been quite a match. I'm sorry I didn't get to see it.*

You feel interested and curious. You remain at the table eating your lunch and enjoy listening to the passionate exchanges. After a while, you begin to join in by asking a question about the score. You chat away with the group until it is time to return to work.

Same scenario, two totally different outcomes because of the different thought patterns.

Thoughts are just thoughts

The second core principle is that our thoughts are just thoughts, *they are not facts.*

Yet often we relate to our thoughts as if they were facts. We accept them unreservedly and rarely challenge them. This means that we give them a lot of power to influence how we feel and, as a result, how we behave.

In fact, our thinking patterns are composed of three layers. The first layer consists of our immediate or automatic thoughts that are so instant we are almost not aware of them. The second layer is composed of the assumptions we make about ourselves, the world and others. The third layer is composed of our set core beliefs about ourselves, others and the world which have been shaped and formed from a very early age. Errors and distortions can occur at all three of these layers, giving rise to a range of negative emotions, including sadness, disappointment, fear and anger, and a range of behaviours that include withdrawal and isolation. Because of the key role our thoughts play in how we feel, it is really important that we are open to challenging them and identifying any bad habits or thinking errors we may have developed but are unaware of.

Faulty thinking patterns

Our awareness and understanding of thinking errors has been influenced by a number of studies on the thinking patterns of people who experience symptoms of depression and anxiety. These studies have found that people can think in ways that are distorted, and that these thinking errors (or 'cognitive distortions') can have a significant negative impact on how these people feel and subsequently behave. This research by leading therapists, such as Aaron T. Beck, Albert Ellis and David Burns[3], has helped to identify a number of the most common thinking-error patterns that keep people stuck because of the range of negative emotions and behaviours they maintain, including despair, low mood, low self-esteem, guilt and hopelessness.

This is really good news because we can now look at the way we think, to see if it contains any of these distorted or negative thinking patterns that may be adversely affecting our mood and sense of well-being.

Listed overleaf are the ten most common thinking errors. See if you recognise any of them.

Top ten thinking errors

1. **Black and white thinking**

   This is also known as 'all or nothing thinking'. An example of this type of thinking error is when you get a B+ in an exam but all you can focus on is the fact that you didn't get an A. You feel like a failure. It is 100 per cent or nothing – there are no grey areas within this thinking pattern and it can cause a lot of pain and disappointment.

2. **Jumping to conclusions**

   This is when you arrive at conclusions about people's attitudes towards you or when you interpret their behaviour with little or no evidence to support your conclusions and interpretations. For example, somebody is late for an appointment with you and you conclude they would rather not meet with you.

3. **Minimisation and magnification**

   This is when you overestimate the significance of everything bad that happens to you and minimise the significance of any good things you experience.

4. **Emotional reasoning**

   Emotional reasoning is the common thinking error of relying on our feelings as evidence of fact – I feel something, therefore it must be true. For example, 'I feel incompetent, therefore I am incompetent', 'I feel ignored or insulted by my friend, therefore she must have ignored or insulted me.'

5. **Mind-reading**

Mind-reading is when you are convinced that you know what other people are thinking, and you usually assume they are thinking negatively about you or judging you. The result is that you then relate to these assumptions as if they were fact and you respond accordingly, both at a feeling level and also in how you behave towards others.

6. **Labelling**

This thinking error leads to a constant negative labelling of yourself. Something bad happens or you experience some disappointment or make a mistake and you respond internally by labelling yourself as incompetent, stupid, a fool, useless or a loser. This type of labelling has a very negative effect on your self-esteem and motivation, and consequently on your mood.

7. **Disqualifying or minimising the positive**

This is the familiar, 'Ah, but ...' error. For example, you receive a compliment from a friend about what you are wearing. You immediately think, 'Ah, but they didn't really mean it, they only said that to be nice'. This has the effect of totally diluting the potentially positive impact of the compliment on your mood. You have successfully batted it away.

8. **Should statements**

'Should' statements are the unwritten rules about your own behaviour and the behaviour of others and they can be quite tyrannical. They can be absolute, as in 'should never' or 'must always', and can leave little room for manoeuvre. For example, 'My home should always be neat and tidy, otherwise I am not a good mother' or 'I should never cry in front of others.'

9. **Overgeneralisation**

Overgeneralisation is a thinking error that occurs when one bad thing happens to us and we draw far-reaching, general conclusions from it. For example, one person lets us down and we conclude, therefore, that no one can be trusted.

10 **Self-blaming**

Self-blaming is about taking responsibility for things that are neither your fault nor your responsibility. For example, your son drops out of college and you immediately blame yourself. You didn't see that coming; you should have said or done something that would have stopped him dropping out.

Identifying your own thinking errors

It is really important that you become familiar with these negative thinking patterns and begin to identify which ones you tend to use. The following exercise will help you do this and will also help you to correct these errors.

In the tables below, identify any examples from your own experience of each of the ten thinking errors and note the impact these distorted thoughts had on your feelings and your behaviour. When you have done this, create a more balanced alternative thought and note how you feel.

Black and white thinking ('all or nothing thinking')

Do you ever give up after one mistake or setback, you think there's no point in going on? Do you ever think you have to achieve 100 per cent or it is just not worth it? You start a diet or exercise programme, make one slip and then you give up because you think all your efforts up to that point are wasted. If so, then you are committing the 'all or nothing thinking' error.

Describe any experiences you have of thinking this way.

Describe the situation/ context	Describe your thought	How did you feel after having this thought?	How did you behave?

Jumping to conclusions

This error is about making conclusions about people's attitudes towards you or interpreting their behaviour with little or no evidence to support your conclusions and interpretations. For some people, jumping to conclusions is the only exercise they ever take! You are making this kind of thinking error if you find yourself predicting or interpreting without evidence. For example, if a friend can't meet up with you at the weekend, then you think that friend doesn't like you or isn't interested in maintaining your friendship. Alternatively, you find yourself not doing something because you 'know' it won't work or it will turn out badly. You predict a negative outcome or experience, and therefore your motivation even to try is compromised.

With this thinking pattern, your feelings respond to the predictions as if they were actually true and, because of this, you are most likely to drop out before you begin.

Have you ever jumped to conclusions?

Describe the situation/ context	Describe your thought	How did you feel after having this thought?	How did you behave?

Minimisation and magnification

This is where you overestimate the significance of everything bad that happens to you and minimise the significance of any good things you experience. When we minimise, phrases like 'it was only', 'it was nothing' and 'I just' become a regular part of our vocabulary. When we magnify, we overstate the significance of the one error we have made and ignore all our other achievements.

Have you ever minimised or maximised an event in your life?

Describe the situation/ context	Describe your thought	How did you feel after having this thought?	How did you behave?

Emotional reasoning

Emotional reasoning is a common thinking error when we rely on our feelings as evidence of fact and don't check out the facts. For example, have you ever found yourself thinking, 'I feel hurt and insulted; therefore, that must have been the intention of the other person?' Another example is, 'I feel stupid; therefore I must be stupid and everyone else must think I am stupid.'

Have there been experiences you have had when you have used your feelings as evidence of fact?

Describe the situation/ context	Describe your thought	How did you feel after having this thought?	How did you behave?

Mind-reading

Mind-reading occurs when you are sure you know what other people are thinking and their alleged thoughts are never positive and frequently contain harsh judgements. When you engage in mind-reading, you behave as if the assumptions you are making about the other person's thoughts are true. You can find yourself saying, 'There's no point; I know what he or she will think', and you adapt your behaviour accordingly.

Describe an occasion where you engaged in mind-reading.

Describe the situation/ context	Describe your thought	How did you feel after having this thought?	How did you behave?

Labelling

This thinking error leads to a constant negative labelling of yourself and others. Something bad happens, you experience some disappointment or make a mistake, and you respond by labelling yourself as incompetent, stupid, a fool, useless or a loser. You respond to other people's mistakes in the same way and label them, which can have serious consequences for the relationship.

Sound familiar? Can you think of any recent examples when you used labelling?

Describe the situation/ context	Describe your thought	How did you feel after having this thought?	How did you behave?

Disqualifying or minimising the positive

If you bat away or minimise anything positive that happens to you, you have engaged in this thinking error. For example, when you don't allow yourself to receive compliments or praise. Do you ever find yourself saying, 'It was nothing' or 'I only ...' in response to praise or a compliment? When you do this, you don't allow yourself to receive the benefit of positive experiences or feedback.

Are there any ways in which you disqualify and minimise the positive?

Describe the situation/ context	Describe your thought	How did you feel after having this thought?	How did you behave?

Should statements

'Should' statements are the unwritten rules about your own behaviour and the behaviour of others. You are making this error when you tell yourself repeatedly that you must do something or be someone and feel bad or guilty when you fail to measure up. 'I should visit my father', 'I should clean my house' or 'I should lose weight' are all familiar 'should' statements. The pressure of the sense of obligation has the opposite effect and demotivates you. 'Should' statements can be quite tyrannical and oppressive and they weigh heavily and leave us with feelings of guilt and disappointment.

Do you have any 'should' statements that weigh you down?

Describe the situation/ context	Describe your thought	How did you feel after having this thought?	How did you behave?

Overgeneralisation

Overgeneralisation is a thinking error that occurs when we make broad general negative conclusions from one disappointing event. We see this one negative event as being part of a pattern and predict that all our experiences will be like this. For example, a friend lets you down and you conclude that you cannot depend on anyone. One person tells you a lie and you conclude that no one can be trusted.

Do you ever overgeneralise?

Describe the situation/ context	Describe your thought	How did you feel after having this thought?	How did you behave?

Self-blaming

Self-blaming is about blaming yourself and taking responsibility for things that are not your fault. You may have some responsibility but when you self-blame, you don't weigh up all the other factors involved. You take all the responsibility and blame yourself, even when others are responsible.

Have you ever assumed responsibility for something that wasn't your fault?

Describe the situation/context	Describe your thought	How did you feel after having this thought?	How did you behave?

Good news!

The good news is that thinking errors are just errors, and errors can be corrected. The following steps will show you ways of doing this.

Six steps to correcting your thinking errors

Now that you are familiar with the various types of thinking errors, the following six-step approach – called the **BRIGHT** method – will help you take control of and change the negative patterns that keep you stuck emotionally.

This method will be especially helpful to you when you notice a significant negative change in your mood.

Step 1: Become aware of any changes in your mood

We feel what we feel because of the way that we think. Therefore when we notice a change in our feelings, it can be a signal to us to take a look at what we are thinking.

Becoming more aware of your feelings involves really tuning in to how you are feeling, and noticing even small changes. At first, these changes may come into your awareness because you notice changes in your body. For example, you might become aware of a sinking feeling in your stomach or you might feel a heaviness in your chest area or a tightness in your throat.

Ask yourself the question: What am I feeling right now? Try and put words on your feelings and, if possible, write them in the box below.

Describe your feelings and how you are in your body

Step 2: Review what has been happening in your life

Sometimes when we have a strong feeling, it can be so powerful that it is hard to make any sense of either it or where it came from.

Ask yourself the following question: Do these feelings I have identified make any sense in terms of what has been happening in my life?

Rewind the tape in your mind and see if you can understand the context for these feelings. You may suddenly make a link; for example, between your change in mood and a comment someone made at a party the evening before or something someone in your life did or did not do last week. When you make any connection between your feelings and what has been happening in your life, make a note of it in your journal.

Step 3: Identify your thoughts that are linked to these feelings

You may need to give this step some time since it can be difficult to unravel your thoughts, especially when these thoughts are often automatic. It may help to consider what you were thinking before you noticed a change in how you were feeling. It may also help to work back from your feeling. For example, if you are aware of feeling sad or angry or disappointed, you might think about what thoughts you had before you started feeling like this.

Researchers in the area of cognitive behavioural therapy have devised a number of questions that can help identify automatic thoughts.[4] These include:

1. What thoughts were going through your mind just before you started to feel like this?
2. If these thoughts were true, what would they say about you?
3. What meaning do these thoughts have for your life and your future?
4. What do they say about the other person?
5. What are you afraid might happen?
6. What is the worst thing that could happen if your thoughts are true?

Write your answers to these questions in the table below.

Questions to help you identify your automatic thoughts

What thoughts were going through your mind just before you started to feel like this?	Before I started feeling this way I was thinking ...
If these thoughts were true, what would they say about you?	If they are true, it would say that I ...
What meaning does it have for your life and your future?	It means ...
What does it say about the other person?	It says ...
What are you afraid might happen?	I am afraid that ...
What is the worst thing that could happen if your thoughts are true?	The worst thing that could happen is ...

Step 4: Give yourself some distance

It is important at this stage to take time out for a minute or two.

Imagine yourself stepping back from the list of thoughts you have identified and just breathing out. You might even imagine yourself walking in a circle around the list of thoughts you have written, just breathing slowly and observing them without judgement.

Step 5: Hold court

Now, you must interrogate these thoughts as if you were the prosecutor in a court of law. Examine each one thoroughly and look for evidence of errors or distortions. Check if any of your thoughts match the common thinking errors listed above.

Look out for any thoughts that contain 'should's or 'ought's or 'must's. It might be helpful to ask some of the following questions about each thought. Write your answers in the table below.

Questions to help you interrogate your thoughts.

Name the thought _____

How do I know this thought is true?	
What is the evidence to say it is true?	
Is it 100 per cent true or only partially true?	
Is there other evidence that suggests it isn't true?	
Am I interpreting?	
Am I mind-reading someone else's thoughts?	
Am I making negative predictions without evidence?	
Am I using my feelings as evidence?	
Am I only concentrating on one aspect of the situation and ignoring other aspects?	

Am I 'catastrophising' – imagining disastrous consequences from something quite small?	
What are the other possible explanations?	
What other outcomes could there be?	

When you have examined your thoughts, identify any thinking errors and write them down by completing a statement that begins with 'I am'. For example, your friend didn't contact you for two weeks. You have a thought that nobody likes you. However, you examine the evidence and find this is not the case and, in fact, there is a lot of evidence to disprove this thought. You name the thinking error and write it down: 'I am overgeneralising.'

Step 6: Think alternative, more balanced thoughts

When you have completed Step 5, take each of the faulty or distorted thoughts you have identified and search for a more realistic, balanced thought or explanation. For example, 'It is not true that nobody likes me. I have many people in my life who care about me. Also, I know my friend cares about me, but she has been busy with her course work for college.'

Now, complete the table overleaf to help you compare the different ways in which your distorted thinking and your rebalanced thinking impact on your feelings.

My initial thought was ...	When I thought this thought, I felt ...	When I examined this thought, I found thinking errors and I am aware that I am [name the thinking error]...	My alternative or re-balanced thought is ...	Whe I thir this n though now fee

After you have practised writing down and examining your thinking patterns, identifying errors and developing more balanced thoughts will become second nature to you.

Take a break now before going on to read the last section on challenging your thinking, which looks at your core beliefs and assumptions.

Assumptions and core beliefs

Our distorted automatic thinking patterns are supported and maintained by the other, deeper layers of our thinking which consist of the assumptions we have about ourselves, the world and others and our core beliefs. Challenging our thinking involves not only looking at our automatic thoughts but also being aware of, and being open to challenging, our assumptions and our core beliefs.

Assumptions are often described as if/then statements and, just like our automatic thoughts, they contain distortions and biases. For example, 'if I don't get an A grade, then my work is useless', 'if people really get to know me, then they won't like me', 'if I trust someone, they will betray me.' They can also contain 'should' statements such as 'men should not show their feelings.'

Can you identify any assumptions you make that contain some biases or distortions?

If _____ then _____

If _____ then _____

If _____ then _____

If _____ then _____

Can you think of any ways these assumptions you have are keeping you stuck in your life or holding you back?

_____

_____

_____

_____

Our assumptions are supported by our core beliefs. These core beliefs are shaped and formed from very early in our lives. They are firmly fixed beliefs about ourselves, the world and others. Some of our core beliefs can contain distortions, such as 'I am unlovable', 'the world is not a safe place', 'people cannot be trusted'. These negative core beliefs about yourself and others may be linked to, and shaped by, life experiences, including trauma. Core beliefs form the deepest layer of our thinking and very often we are not even aware of them. However, if you notice a theme or a pattern in your distorted automatic thoughts that constantly reoccurs, this may help you identify an underlying core belief of which you may not be aware.

There is a simple technique that will help you identify the core beliefs you have about yourself. It is called the downward arrow technique,[5] and it involves repeatedly asking the question, 'If this were true, what does this say about me?', until you arrive at your core belief. Have a look at the following example.

Your friend Brian told you he would drop in on his way home from work.

He didn't arrive and he didn't call you.

You feel hurt.

Your automatic thought is: *He doesn't like me.*
(Q. If this were true, what does it say about me?)

It says nobody likes me.
(Q. If this were true what does it say about me?)

It says I will never have any friends.
(Q. If this were true, what does it say about me?)

It says I will always be lonely.
(Q. If this were true, what does it say about me?)

It says I am unlovable.

In the space opposite, practise using this technique to identify any core beliefs you have that might be keeping you stuck emotionally in your life. Think of something that has happened that upset you.

Describe the situation or event.

_____

_____

Describe your feeling.

_____

_____

Name your automatic thought.

_____

_____

(Q. If this were true, what does it say about me?)

↓

It says

_____

_____

(Q. If this were true, what does it say about me?)

↓

It says

_____

(Q. If this were true, what does it say about me?)

↓

It says

(Q. If this were true, what does it say about me?)

↓

It says

Challenging your core beliefs

Once you have identified your core beliefs, you can begin to understand and challenge them. However, because they are deeply held, they are not easy to challenge but there are a number of questions you can ask yourself that will help you do this.[6]

Below are some questions to help you challenge your core beliefs. Complete this exercise for each of the core beliefs you have identified.

Name the belief _____

When I take into account all my life experience, what evidence is there to suggest that this belief is true?	
Has this belief always been true for me?	
Does this belief look at the whole picture? Are there other aspects that need to be taken into account?	
Does this belief help me to feel good about myself or does it have the opposite effect?	
Is this a belief I have chosen myself or has it been shaped and influenced by my experiences growing up?	

The answers to these questions can generate strong counter-arguments that weaken the grip of distorted core beliefs. Positive affirmations also provide an important counterbalance to distorted core beliefs. In the next chapter, we will show you how to develop and use affirmations in your life to generate positive self-belief and undermine negative self-talk. Over time, you will be able to identify and replace distorted core beliefs with positive, more balanced ones.

Well done! You have taken on the challenge of challenging your thinking. This is not an easy task but a very important step towards changing the way you think and feel. The work you have just done shows how committed you are to achieving your goal of leading a fuller and a happier life.

Pathway Four
Talk Back to Negative Self-Talk

Who said,
'You can't, won't, never will?'
Who said,
'Praise is poison,
speaking well of yourself is pride?
You must think, talk and be this way
because this is who you are?'
Who said,
'They did
and now I do, because it's the only language I know?'
Who said?

Most of us learned early in our lives not to speak well of ourselves. If we did, we were branded as big-headed, cocky or full of ourselves.

However, if praise was in short supply, then there was no shortage of negative input. People seemed to queue up to 'put us in our place' and 'take us down a peg'. Those people usually had power, like parents and teachers, and what they said often made a deep impression on us.

While a good word shines a light on and nurtures a young self-image, a negative word or label diminishes that self-image and causes us to doubt ourselves. The seeds of self-doubt and self-criticism begin to germinate and, over time, this negativity becomes internalised and forms part of our self-view. Almost unconsciously, we become our own best self-critic, constantly and consistently undermining our self-belief and confidence. In fact, this process becomes a self-perpetuating, downward spiral – research shows that people who feel down and have low self-esteem filter out any information that disproves their negative view of themselves. They pay more attention to information that confirms their own negative perception or evaluation.

Negative self-statements

Tick any of the following negative self-statements that sound familiar to you.

I am not good enough	
I am useless	
I am boring	
I am too thin	
I am too fat	
I look awful	
I am not bright enough	
I am incompetent	
I am weak	
I am too emotional	
I am not popular	
I am stupid	
I should be a better cook	

I should be a better ... father/son/mother/sister	
I failed	
I can't	
It's my fault	
I never get things right	
I embarrassed myself	
There's no point	

How many of the twenty did you tick? In most cases, we are not even aware of our negative self-statements because they have become automatic and we don't stop to question them.

Take a moment to consider the negative self-statements you use most often about yourself to yourself.

Do you compare yourself negatively to others? Do you judge yourself harshly? In writing your answers below, consider how you relate to yourself in all the different areas of your life and in the different roles you have, e.g. work, relationships and family.

Top three negative self-statements

1. _____

2. _____

3. _____

Did anything surprise you about your list?

Take a moment to read aloud the negative statements you have written.

What is it like to hear these statements? What feelings do they leave you with?

When I hear these statements, I feel _____

_____

_____

_____

_____

_____

If somebody else spoke to you like this, what would you feel and what would you say to that person?

_____

_____

_____

_____

_____

Successful people don't talk themselves down. Think of a successful, confident person with a strong self-belief. It can be someone you know or a famous person. How do you know they are confident? List some of the things about them that lead you to think they are confident and believe in themselves.

_____

_____

_____

_____

_____

Now imagine some of the positive self-statements a successful person might say to themselves.

They would say _____

_____

_____

_____

_____

_____

Undermining the power of negative self-talk

Negative self-statements are very comfortable where they are. They like the position of authority they hold over us and are not willing to give up that position easily. Why would they? The following three-step approach will help you to undermine their power and counteract the negative influence they have in your life.

Step 1: Increase your awareness

The first step to defeating negative self-talk is to become more aware of your own particular pattern of negativity and to catch yourself just before you put yourself down. This may not be as easy as it seems because these negative self-statements will have become so automatic that you are probably not even aware they exist.

Look for clues of their presence from changes in your body. Perhaps you notice a sinking feeling or a heaviness in your body. You might become aware of a change in your mood, a feeling of disappointment, of hopelessness or despair, or you might notice a change in your behaviour. For example, do you ever want to avoid going somewhere you had been planning to go or avoid meeting someone you had been looking forward to meeting? Try to name the negative self-statement that gave rise to this feeling or change in behaviour. Check the list you have written of your most common negative self-statements and see if any of these are present.

Step 2: Challenge your negative self-statements

Your negative self-statements retain their power over you only because they have never been challenged. Imagine that you are Sherlock Holmes and that every negative self-statement you make has to be put under the microscope and examined carefully for evidence, as if you are preparing for a court of law.

Take your top three negative self-statements and write them in the table below; then, for each statement, answer the questions listed.

Top three negative self-statements

	1.	2.	3.
Negative self-statement			

What is the evidence to support this statement?			
What is the evidence that does not support it?			
Is it 100 per cent true or only partially true?			
What are the alternative statements?			
If I asked someone close to me about this statement, what would they say?			

What was it like to do this exercise? Did anything surprise you?

_____

_____

_____

Step 3: Counter-attack with positive affirmations

A really effective way to undermine the power of negative self-statements is to replace them with their opponents. Begin to actively affirm yourself by creating a list of positive self-statements, which are also called affirmations.

These statements work in the opposite way to negative self-talk. If this sounds alien to you and you are wondering if it could possibly work, just ask yourself the following question: Has years of putting yourself down and criticising yourself been effective in eroding your self-esteem and undermining your confidence? If the answer is yes, then it stands to reason that the opposite can also apply. Writing down and reading positive affirmations aloud will help to re-programme the way you think.

Habits don't start as habits. They begin as actions and, as we perform them over and over again, they become 'second nature' to us; that is, habitual. Remember when you first tied your shoelaces and were short a thumb? Remember the first time you rode a bike and looked at the front tyre with Zen-like concentration? You do these things now, without thinking, because you've done them thousands of times since. When the affirmations have started to change the way you think, the positive response, the good word, will stop seeming 'artificial' and become integrated into your everyday vocabulary.

Try it!

Below are some tips to help you develop your own list of positive affirmations.

Affirmations work best when they:
- begin with 'I'
- are short, simple statements you can really own
- are positive and contain no negatives
- are in the present tense.

Positive self-statements

Try and compile your own list of fifteen positive self-statements using the following openings:

- *I am ...*
- *I can ...*
- *I am learning to ...*
- *I have ...*
- *I am beginning to ...*
- *I believe that I ...*

If you are finding this difficult, ask someone you trust to help you complete the exercise.

The following list of affirmations may also help you if you get stuck.

I work hard.

I am a kind person.

I am learning to trust myself.

I have a good sense of humour.

I am beginning to feel hopeful.

I am a good neighbour.

I am a caring person.

I have a nice smile.

I have a warm personality.

I am becoming more optimistic.

I am a loyal friend.

I am creative.

I am responsible.

I am learning to take risks.

I am open-minded.

I am musical.

I am intelligent.

I am attractive.

I have a nice figure.

I am strong.
I am learning to accept myself.
I am gentle.
I am considerate.
I am determined.
I am talented.
I am sexy.
I have good friends.
I am curious.
I am a good parent.
I am forgiving.
I am respectful.
I am trustworthy.
I am loving.
I enjoy a challenge.
I am playful.
I am becoming more confident.
I am beginning to accept myself.
I am open to possibilities.
I am dedicated.
I am reliable.

In the space overleaf, write the fifteen affirmations you have chosen.
Remember, only write down an affirmation if you believe it about
yourself. This doesn't mean you have to believe in it 100 per cent or
that you have to believe you are like this 100 per cent of the time.

(This would be an 'all or nothing' thinking error!) What it does mean is that you are open to acknowledging and nurturing these different positive aspects of who you are.

Fifteen positive statements about myself that I believe:

1. _____

2. _____

3. _____

4. _____

5. _____

6. _____

7. _____

8. _____

9. _____

10. _____

11. _____

12. _____

13. _____

14. _____

15. _____

When you have completed the list, take a moment to read each statement aloud. Read the affirmations slowly and leave a five- or six-second pause between each one. Synchronise your breathing with the affirmations, breathing in as you read the affirmation and repeating each affirmation as you breathe out. Now, speak each affirmation aloud. Speak each affirmation with feeling, rather than just reciting it. This will help your heart as well as your head connect with and own the affirmation.

Make a note in your journal of what it feels like for you to acknowledge to yourself these different aspects of who you are.

How to use your affirmations

Affirmations are not meant to be written on a list and forgotten. They are meant to be spoken aloud regularly until they become integrated into your active sense of who you are. It takes about three positive self-statements to counteract the influence of every negative self-statement, so it is important to use your affirmations on a daily basis.

Plan how you will do this. Why not set a particular time aside each morning and evening to read them aloud? Perhaps it might help to leave the list beside your bed, so that you can read them first thing in the morning and last thing at night. You might speak the affirmations into a digital recorder or mobile phone and listen back on your headphones while travelling to work or to the shops. You might take one particular affirmation and work with it for a day, repeating it to yourself or incorporating it into a meditation.

Find a way to use your affirmations which works for you. At the end of each month, review your list and see if there are any additional affirmations you would like to add.

Why not start now?

Pathway Five

Let Laughter In

The American tourist found a small café tucked into a tiny lane in Cork city. The proprietress was a timid, harried woman who was trying to keep the place one step above botulism and the choice of the day was, 'Take it or leave it.'

'Honey,' he declared, 'I'll have the Caesar salad, heavy on the Parmesan. I'll have a sixteen-ounce rare steak with pepper sauce. Gimme a side order of dauphinoise potatoes and steamed vegetables with that. For dessert, I'll have crème brûlée and for drinks, how about a bottle of Margaux. Ya got all that?'

'If we had all that,' she said wistfully, 'we'd ate it ourselves.'

Humour comes in many shapes and forms, from smiling to belly-aching laughter, from verbal puns to self-deprecating witty comments, from playfulness to practical jokes. The ancient Greeks believed that there were liquids, balanced like ballast tanks, in various parts of our bodies which affected our moods. They considered it was vital for a person's mental well-being to keep these liquids balanced – too much or too little of one or another could lead to either euphoria or melancholy.

Many studies show that humour and laughter can have a positive effect on our sense of well-being and mood. We feel better, even if only for a short while, after a good laugh. When we smile, a subtle change takes place in our perception of the world.

There are also physical benefits because laughter sets off a chain reaction in the body, reducing stress and tension. Humour can help to boost your immune system and alleviate symptoms of anxiety. It is not possible to laugh and feel anxious at the same time. This ability to see the funny, absurd, bizarre and ridiculous side of any situation is one of the things that distinguishes us from other creatures.

The father of the bride had cherished his daughter for thirty years and insisted on including a memory from every one of those years in his wedding speech. One of his own brothers had drunk 'not wisely but too well' and could no longer endure the boredom. He called the waiter. 'I'll give you fifty quid if you'll go up there and knock him out.'

'I'll do it for nothing,' the waiter replied.

The waiter sneaked around behind the father and waited his chance. During a smattering of polite applause, he made his move – but missed the speaker and clocked the father of the groom, who toppled under the table.

The bride's father continued as if nothing had happened until a voice from under the table said, 'Hit me again, I can still hear him.'

Humour takes us out of ourselves. Our sense of humour is like a psychological Swiss army knife that is available to us as a powerful resource. We can draw on it to help us cope with difficult challenges, including loss and disappointment. It can help us to build and repair relationships, and to enhance our sense of well-being and self-esteem. When we can joke about ourselves, it serves to keep us grounded and prevents us from taking ourselves too seriously.. If you can connect with your playful side, it will help reduce stress and you will feel less overwhelmed. Allowing yourself to reconnect with your playful, flirtatious side in your relationships can help nurture and enhance these relationships.

Disaster has the potential either to enclose the spirit or to free it. It can refocus us on the essential things, like life and love. People have worked for many years, been devastated when they have lost their jobs, but have returned home to rediscover their real reason for living – like the man who took his mother walking on the beach to tell her he was leaving the priesthood and was amazed when she responded, 'Is that all? I was so terribly worried that you were sick.' Focused on what he considered to be his failure, he had lost sight of the breadth of his mother's love. Our roles can so easily distance us from ourselves and our relationships, but when the role becomes containing, a breakdown can become the prelude to a more qualitative life.

But humour is a two-edged sword! In politics, it can be used to devastating effect. Jonathan Swift's satires punctured the pomposity of those in power and were proof positive that the 'pen is mightier than the sword'. The putdowns in parliamentary debate are quoted long after the worthy speeches are forgotten. But humour can also be defensive, reductive and caustic. Humour can be used as a barrier to intimacy, a way of keeping others 'at arm's length' and of shielding ourselves against self-revelation. But if you use this kind of humour over a period of time, it can isolate you and alienate others. Put-downs are long remembered and rarely appreciated by those who are at the receiving end of them. Too many adults have painful memories of the sarcastic remarks made by family and teachers.

There is a large body of evidence to support the belief that a rich vein of humour emerged among those held in concentration camps and other places where humans were being treated savagely. Much of that humour was a method of ridiculing the inflated self-image of the captors while proclaiming and defending the unbreakable spirit of the captives. It also promoted solidarity among the suffering and a sense that there was more to life and them than their horrific circumstances. Laughter in this type of context is a symptom of hope, a belief that there is a better way and that things can be different.

Paddy and Jack decided to make their fortune in America in the hope that things could be different for them. It was the era of the Wild West, when fortunes could be made in gold, and so they headed west. They were the only entrepreneurs in the history of the time who started at the bottom and went down.

Finally, when they had deserted the wagon and eaten the mule, they staggered into a small town. A notice pinned to the sheriff's door promised a five-dollar bounty for Indian feathers. Back the pair went to the prairie, where they mugged an Indian and cashed in on his feathers.

When the bounty had been imbibed, they repaired to the prairie to sleep it off. As dawn broke, Paddy opened a bleary eye to find they were surrounded by a large party of angry Indians in full war bonnets. 'Jack,' he whispered, delightedly, 'wake up, lad, we're rich.'

Over the years, I have presented many lectures and courses on bereavement and loss. I try to pepper my lectures on serious and challenging topics with humorous anecdotes.

Recently, at the end of a lecture given to a local community, a lady approached and said, 'I laughed so much tonight. The last series of lectures was on marriage and I didn't laugh even once!' Don't get distracted by wondering why she found marriage unfunny; consider the appropriateness of humour in a lecture on bereavement.

We believe that people who laugh relax, listen better and absorb more. And there is a lot of research that points to the fact that people who laugh release tension, are less aggressive and irritable, and are more relaxed and open. In fact, humour can help facilitate the processing of grief.

'Do you think bereavement is funny?' a radio interviewer once asked. 'What do the bereaved have to laugh about? Won't some people think you're making fun or light of their pain?'

These were really good questions. Bereavement and loss are not funny, but you might say that things can be fatal without being serious. Part of the process of grieving involves rediscovering the whole person and the depth and breadth of our relationship with them. It means looking at the person you've lost, the real person, with all their faults, foibles, gifts and irritating qualities.

Bereavement is a change in a relationship, and joy, loss, pain and, yes, humour are part of that changing relationship. When people remember, they remember light and shade. We can take something seriously without erasing the light from it. The bereaved can have things to laugh about and that laughter can be healing. I was talking recently to a man who was laughing heartily while sharing a story about his son who had died tragically. He stopped suddenly and remarked, 'Listen to me laughing!' Why should guilt be attached to the laughter that comes from warm memories? In bereavement, laughter and tears come from the same source and are equally appropriate ways of grieving a relationship.

Laughter needn't be interpreted as trivialising grief. In fact, it can acknowledge and express the full, rounded character of the person who has died and the breadth of our relationship with that person. I remember Linda and I laughing heartily at my brother's funeral in New York when we discovered that his golfing buddies had placed a left-handed golf club in his coffin knowing full well that he was a right-handed player and would have appreciated the joke.

It can be difficult to see the 'funny side' of a disaster because disasters tend to explode, like supernovas, and blind us to other dimensions.

We all have ambitions that are never realised, dreams that turn to dust. Our natural response is to feel disappointed, disillusioned and defeated. Such realities are no laughing matter in the short term. A favourite book of ours is *Zorba the Greek* by Nikos Kazantzakis, which was released as a movie starring Anthony Quinn. It's the story of a young Englishman who goes to a Greek island and hires Zorba as his guide. The young man dreams of transforming the lives of the islanders by erecting a system of pylons and cables that will transport the ore from the mountain mine to the port below. Of course, the real story traces the relationship between the 'uptight' young man and his life-loving companion. After many trials and adventures, the system is finally put in place and the islanders gather for its inauguration. As the Orthodox priest blesses the pylons, they topple like dominos down the mountainside and everything is ruined. In the shocked silence that follows the last crash, Zorba turns to his young friend and says, 'Now, I will teach you to dance.'

Your sense of humour can be the spark among the embers that reignites your passion for life and teaches you to dance.

Bringing laughter back into your life

When we are feeling down, we tend to filter out everything in our life that is inconsistent with our mood. Yet humour can be an important resource to help you move out of the dark place in which you are stuck. Can you imagine what it might feel like if you could bring some laughter back into your life? That may seem like a giant step from where you are at the moment, but you don't have to go too far from home to begin to take the first step.

We all have our favourite humorous television shows or films – ours are the episode in *Friends* where Joey gets his head stuck in the turkey, and any episode of *Fawlty Towers*.

What is your favourite comedy show or film? What parts make you laugh?

_____

_____

_____

_____

Take a moment to recall your favourite comedians. What is it about them that makes you laugh? Is it their timing, their material, the way they walk, the way they look?

_____

_____

_____

_____

_____

_____

What is your experience of being playful? Were you playful as a child or do you have any memories of being around someone who was playful? Describe what that experience was like.

_____

_____

_____

_____

Try to imagine what it might be like if you could allow yourself to be more playful in the different areas of your life – home, work, relationships and friendships. What might that look and feel like? How would you like to behave if you were to allow yourself to be more playful and didn't hold yourself back?

_____

_____

_____

_____

What makes you smile?

We all have a treasure trove of memories that make us smile when we bring them to mind, no matter where we are.

> **Below are some of the memories that make us smile.**
>
> - Our son writing an essay about his family when he was about eight, that included the line 'My dad has grey hair but I don't mind.'
> - A memory of dividing a candy bar with my brother when I was about nine. I broke the bar into two uneven pieces and held them up for his inspection. 'They're not even, are they?' I asked. 'No.' Then I bit a piece from the bigger bit to make them even and he accepted the other.
> - A boy in my class reading out his English essay which began with: 'One day, me and two other dogs went out hunting.'
> - Telling our six-year-old that our friends were going to have a new baby, and him replying, 'But what will they do with the old one?'
> - We both smile when we remember spending a couple of hours trading puns early on in our relationship and the peals of laughter between us as the puns went from bad to worse, or sitting in a yellow vintage car in the snow on our wedding day while the driver hastily tried to change a tyre.

What are the memories that make you smile? Take a moment to consider them and write down what comes to mind.

_____

_____

_____

_____

_____

_____

There are a number of practical things you can do to help you reconnect with your sense of humour and keep that spark alive in your life.

You could:

- get together a collection of CDs or DVDs of your favourite funny shows and set some time aside each week to view or listen to one of them
- set up a regular comedy evening where you invite some friends around to watch a humorous show or film
- make a collection of your favourite jokes, write them in a notebook and keep that with you to reread when you need cheering up
- make a list in your journal of all the things that make you smile and regularly update that list when something else happens that made you smile
- when you are feeling stressed, try to step back for a moment and see if you can find the funny side of the situation
- share your jokes – tell your favourite joke to a friend or work colleague

- try to nurture your playful side in your relationships with your partner or friends – allow yourself to take a risk.

Why not start by doing just one of the suggestions listed? Pick the suggestion that you feel would be easiest for you to begin with. Go for it. You have nothing to lose and you might have some fun along the way!

Just to encourage you, here is one last tall tale ...

John had been a policeman for thirty years before he finally plucked up the courage to sit the sergeant's examination. Suddenly, he found himself surrounded by younger models with incredible qualifications.

The examination paper didn't help.

Question one read:

You are on traffic duty when two vehicles collide. The vehicle 90 per cent in the wrong is being driven by the superintendent's wife. Just then, a well-known criminal rides by on a bicycle as a woman screams for help (childbirth has been induced by the excitement). Just then a swimmer calls for help from the river. What would you do?

After scratching his head for twenty minutes, he wrote: *I would take off my uniform and mingle with the crowd.*

Pathway Six

Speak from the Heart

When it was time to choose subjects for my final exams, I was one short. Careers guidance, in my day, meant asking a fellow student for advice – an example of the cross-fertilisation of ignorance.

'Do Art,' the sage said, 'any idiot could pass Art.'

Who could resist such a recommendation? I joined a group who had been studying Art – seemingly from the cradle. And so I shared the Art room with sawn-off versions of Monet, Picasso and Modigliani. Art was not my forte – my still-life was still moving at the end of the lesson. During first term, I went through my 'Blue Period' because it was the only colour pencil I had.

Our teacher was an elderly, soft-spoken man who enthused about framing, shading, perspective and many other mysterious concepts. I remember he set us a task, and then came around to check on our progress. He showered praise on a whole line of artists and then he came to me. I could have argued that the jumble of lines on the paper was an abstract, thoughtful and challenging depiction of the vase and flower, but I knew a lost cause when I saw one. He hummed, for a while, and then patted my shoulder and said, 'Very brave, Christy.'

There is an art in giving compliments and the good artist never 'gilds the lily', shading a compliment from fair to flattery. The practitioner must also have an eye for the essential; the overall effort rather than the perfection of the portrait, the single thing done well, rather than the many flaws. Looking back, I see my Art teacher as an impressionist, someone who can give weight and colour to a single dot on a canvas – or on a boy.

There is a very beautiful proverb which says: 'Whatever is spoken from the heart speaks to the heart.' A compliment spoken from the heart shines a light on whatever is good within us, and whatever the light shines upon will grow. Shining a light on the gift of another person nurtures their gift and their appreciation of the giver.

Instinctively, we lavish praise on babies, sometimes for the most disgusting reasons.

'Who's a great boy or girl then?' we whoop when they produce a nappy that qualifies as hazardous material. They throw up all over us and we say, 'Better up than down.' As babies develop, we keep up a running commentary of praise as they move from sitting, to crawling, to toddling, walking and talking. We seem to know instinctively that they will need this kind of nourishment if they are to grow strong in themselves and confident in their abilities.

Hope is built on a foundation of achievement. Compliments affirm, or 'bed in', our own awareness of our abilities and potential so that we develop the confidence to build towards our goals and realise that potential.

Paying someone a compliment is an investment in their giftedness and adds another building block to their self-confidence.

Many of us will recall a parent, relative, friend or teacher who had the gift of 'the good word'. Maybe they stayed in our memories because we encountered so much criticism or so little encouragement from others that their kind words stood out. Many people have a multiple of negative memories for every positive one; memories of being assured that they 'would never amount to anything'.

The 'good word' is a seed that can root and grow in the unlikeliest soil. Every time we care enough to compliment something good in another, we give sunlight, oxygen and water to that seed. Flowers have bloomed in the unlikeliest environments.

We flew over the Sahara once. From a plane, it's like an endless beach that rolls on and on, bare and barren. Rain rarely falls there but, when it does, flowers bloom and carpet the sand. A person's gift may be buried in arid soil for years, simply waiting for the right word from the right person.

A successful businessman once confided to me that his childhood had been blighted by neglect. His father had drunk to excess and his mother was so busy holding it all together for him and his siblings that she never had time to nourish her son's dreams.

'I grew up hungry for attention,' he said. 'That kind of hunger can lead a boy to trouble because trouble always gets attention.'

'What helped you turn your life around?' I asked.

'A teacher,' he answered. 'He wasn't even my teacher but I met him almost every day when I crossed the schoolyard. And every day without fail, he said something complimentary or encouraging to me before we parted. That man saw something in me; something different to the trouble everybody else saw. I began to believe things could be different – I could be different. I began to see that if I gave the same energy to study as I was giving to mischief, I could make something of myself. My only regret is that I never told him what an important part he played in my life.'

Every time we meet another human being, it is an opportunity to reflect their beauty, worth and giftedness to them. What a power for good and an opportunity for growth that is.

When I was a child, I loved finding dandelions that had gone to seed. Each dandelion wore a bonnet of white, winged seeds and, when I blew on them, they lifted to soar and scatter on the wind. *Where did they go?* I wondered. *Where did they land and root and grow?* Compliments are the seeds we give breath to. They cost us no more than a little breath to send them winging into the hearts of man, woman or child, and what a difference they can make.

Yet we can be shy about giving compliments and hold ourselves back. There are a number of reasons why we talk ourselves out of being more complimentary.

One reason is that we can convince ourselves that compliments are unnecessary.

'They should know that I appreciate them without being told. After all, I do so many things that show my appreciation.' While actions can 'speak louder than words', many people who have enjoyed long and harmonious relations will say, 'A little thanks never goes astray.'

But it's more than that.

Compliments aren't an afterthought in a relationship. They are not an extra but an integral part of the ongoing building of a relationship. In that sense, they may not be the solid foundations, roof or walls, but they are the mortar that binds us closer together.

We can also worry about being misinterpreted or get overly concerned about embarrassing the other person. Yes, some people can feel embarrassed by a compliment, possibly because they're not accustomed to being complimented. Perhaps these people need compliments more than others. Any positive thing we feel like saying or doing shouldn't depend on the other person's possible reaction. They have the responsibility for how they receive it.

What is your experience of giving compliments? Do you find it easy or difficult to give compliments?

_____

_____

Describe the last time you gave someone a compliment. Recall what you said and to whom.

_____

_____

_____

_____

_____

How did you feel after you had given the compliment?

_____

_____

_____

_____

_____

Which type of compliment do you think would be easier for you to give and which one would challenge you the most?

Would it be easier for you to:

- *compliment someone on something that they were wearing*

or

- *compliment someone on something they had achieved*

or

- *compliment someone on a personal quality of theirs, such as their warmth or ability to listen?*

_____

_____

_____

_____

_____

Receiving compliments

Unfortunately, we don't always receive compliments graciously.

I envy Americans. You give them a compliment and they actually take it! They smile and say 'thank you' and the cycle of giving and receiving is completed. We Irish, on the other hand, don't do compliments. Despite the Irish proverb which translates into, 'Praise youth and youth will flower', we are adept at deflecting the compliment and suspecting the giver.

'Your blouse is lovely.'

'I've had this old thing for years.'

'Your hair is really nice.'

'Okay, you crashed the car, didn't you?'

When did we decide we were unworthy of compliments?

The word 'compliment' has 'to fulfil' at its root.

When someone reflects something good or beautiful about us to ourselves and we refuse to accept it, we are cutting off a pathway to our own sense of fullness and completeness. At the same time, we are also sending a message to the giver that we are not open to receiving nourishment from them.

In our culture, to be 'fulfilled' is often interpreted, negatively, as to be 'full of yourself', vain, boastful or self-regarding – 'talking yourself up' was always taboo; 'talking yourself down' was both a virtue and a hobby. Gifts, talents and abilities were never to be acknowledged or declared, and so we denied them. Sadly, the gift that is denied withers and leaves a hole in the spirit. That hole can become a black hole that sucks down the light from the space around it.

Being open to the process of giving and receiving compliments is an important way to build positive emotional experiences that can enhance your sense of well-being and self-esteem and also strengthen your emotional connections with other people.

What is your experience of receiving compliments?

Do you remember receiving a compliment at any stage in your life that stayed with you and made a difference? Take a moment to describe the experience. How old were you? Who gave you the compliment? What was said? What did it feel like for you?

_____

_____

_____

_____

_____

How do you receive compliments?

If we receive a compliment, we allow ourselves to receive nourishment from another person. It helps us to feel good about ourselves and builds our self-confidence.

Try to recall the last time you received a compliment. It could have been a comment about your appearance, something you were wearing, your work or an achievement. Describe the compliment and who gave it to you.

_____

_____

_____

_____

_____

How did you feel when you heard the compliment?

_____

_____

_____

_____

_____

Describe how you responded. Did you receive the compliment or did you push it away, deny it or minimise it?

_____

_____

_____

_____

_____

If you did push away the compliment, what do you think that was like for the person who gave you the compliment?

_____

_____

_____

_____

_____

Describe some other ways you could have received the compliment?

_____

_____

_____

_____

_____

Complimenting yourself

Do you ever compliment yourself for how you look or things that you have achieved?

Look in a mirror and find one thing, however small, to genuinely compliment yourself on – it could be your eyes, your teeth, what you are wearing. Make a note of what it feels like to compliment yourself.

_____

_____

_____

_____

_____

Take the compliments challenge

Set yourself the task of giving at least two compliments a day – one to someone else and one to yourself. Try to vary the type of compliments you give and include ones that are more personal.

When you give a compliment, try to make eye contact with the person and be aware of your body language and the tone of your voice.

Record the compliments you give at the end of each day in your journal.

Become aware of how you receive compliments – try to catch yourself before you bat them away and allow yourself to receive them fully. Record these in your journal and note how you feel.

A true compliment is a rare and extraordinary thing. We are struck by a profile, stilled by a talent, moved by an unconscious grace – and something in our soul responds. Something deep down in the untainted, untutored part of ourselves recognises and responds to that deep and beautiful part of another. In that mutual recognition of giftedness, gifts are exchanged and, in that process, both are enriched.

Pathway Seven

Worry Your Worries

I climbed trees when I was a boy, but never to the top. It looked a little slender up there and my natural caution confined me to the lower branches. It was bliss; feeling the warm, rough bark, smelling the resin, hearing the wind sieving through the leaves and seeing the world from a different perspective.

What goes around comes around.

Our younger son inherited the tree-climbing gene but skipped the caution one. Every tree had to be conquered; there was no place like the top. Cautionary tales of tumbling fell on deaf ears. 'It's a bushy tree,' he reasoned; 'some branch is bound to catch me on the way down.' We didn't want to spoil his pleasure but we didn't want him to discover the painful reality of gravity either.

We took turns on tree-watch, standing at the base calling warnings and advice to the little head that looked a lot littler from where we stood. Then a friend advised us to make a checklist.

'Check his sense of safety and what he'll do in an

emergency,' she said. 'If that doesn't work for you, climb up to a level you're comfortable with and share his experience. You'll be near enough to advise or catch, and high enough to enjoy his "high".'

It worked – over time. That time gave him the chance to grow stronger and more confident. It also taught him tree-craft; testing branches before trusting them with his weight and anchoring his hands before moving his feet.

Would you describe yourself as a worrier? If you answered yes, then would you also describe yourself as a creative person? It might surprise you to know that this capacity you have to worry comes from a very creative place within you – the place of poetry and art.

It is a uniquely human gift to be able to move out of the present moment and imagine likely future events or outcomes. The ability to dream and imagine is very powerful and exciting. What a gift! However, if you find that your thinking ahead always anticipates negative events or consequences, then you run the risk of becoming stuck in a paralysing negative cycle of worry and fear.

This cycle works in the following way. You think about a future event, such as going to a party. You predict that something bad or upsetting will happen. As part of this creative process of prediction, you experience the event as if it is happening, or has actually happened. You then begin, almost simultaneously, to experience some of the emotions that you would feel if your prediction came true – powerful emotions, such as sadness, disappointment, dread or shame. These strong feelings, like all feelings, are experienced in the body and the body has a way of making itself heard. Suddenly, you become aware of a tightness in your stomach or the rapidity of your heartbeat. Your legs feel shaky or your palms become sweaty. This awareness creates a further layer of worry as you interpret your bodily sensations as evidence that your predictions are accurate. The overall effect is paralysing.

Worry wears the one who worries.

Worry cripples the human spirit and restricts potential. It sucks the life out of living. A worried person can feel like an animal trapped in a cage, walking the same space over and over, round and round, burning energy and getting nowhere.

The word 'worry' comes from an Old English word which means 'to harm'. Think of how many times you have heard someone say, 'I'm worried sick' or 'She was worn away with worry' or 'He worried himself into his grave.'

Constant, unremitting worry can enclose us and trap us inside ourselves, so that we haven't the time, energy or inclination to relate to the important people in our lives. You could say that we raise the drawbridge, lock ourselves in a tower, cut off our supply of nourishment from others and become debilitated.

In this chapter, we will help you to break this restrictive cycle of worry and become more open to possibilities and joy in your life.

9 Practical Steps to Help You Overcome Your Anxiety

1. Begin to worry your worry
2. Befriend your worries
3. Count the cost
4. Investigate your worry
5. Limit the time you spend worrying
6. Avoid avoidance
7. Work with your breathing
8. Harness the energy of worry
9. Practise relaxation

1. Begin to worry your worry

Worrying is an internal process that we often keep hidden from others. The person opposite you on the bus gazing out the window has no awareness of the torrent of anxiety that is coursing through your blood and cannot hear the sound of your heart pounding. Worry, like a mushroom, thrives in a hidden, dark environment. Therefore, the first step to overcoming your anxiety is to begin to *worry your worry* by opening the door and letting some light in.

How can you do this?

There are a number of steps that can help you. The first is to name your worries – write them down. This process, which is called externalisation, moves your worries from the inside, where they have free rein to run riot inside your mind and your body, to the outside, where you can begin to look at and deal with them.

In the space below, make a list of the five main things you have worried about in the past few weeks.

In the past few weeks, I have worried that:

1. _____

2. _____

3. _____

4. _____

5 _____

Ask yourself if there is a pattern to your worry. Do you worry more about bad things happening to yourself or to others? Do you worry about practical things like money, paying bills, etc? Do you worry about what other people might say or think about you?

My worrying is mostly about _____

_____

_____

For each of the five worries you listed above, ask yourself what needs to happen for you to stop worrying.

1. *I would no longer need to worry about* _____

    if _____

    _____

2. *I would no longer need to worry about* _____

    if _____

    _____

3. *I would no longer need to worry about* _____

    if _____

    _____

4.   *I would no longer need to worry about* _____

      if _____

      _____

5.   *I would no longer need to worry about* _____

      if _____

      _____

2. Befriend your worries

The idea of befriending your worries might sound strange to you. What we mean by 'befriending' is getting to know your worry deeply, not just in terms of its symptoms and how it expresses itself, but in terms of its history.

Can you begin to show some compassion towards your worry? Ask yourself the following questions:

Do your worries make any sense in terms of your life history?

_____

_____

_____

What does your worry need?

_____

_____

_____

What would your worry say if it could speak?

In order to consider this, it might be useful to imagine your worry sitting opposite you in a chair. Imagine yourself asking it what it feels like to worry all the time. Imagine yourself asking your worry what it needs in order to find peace.

_____

_____

_____

Take a moment to write down any insights or responses that come to you after doing this exercise.

_____

_____

_____

_____

_____

_____

3. Count the cost

Worry does not come cheaply. It demands attention and exacts a high price in time and energy. Have you ever considered what your worry is costing you? Consider the amount of time that could be spent with friends or family, the pressure on your relationships, as well as the physical and emotional energy that your worrying consumes. Take a moment to count the cost of your worry.

The energy and time I spend worrying stops me from:

1. _____

2. _____

3. _____

4. _____

5. _____

Imagine the possibilities that could open up for you if you harnessed this worrying energy and redirected it in a way that would give you more options in your life.

If I didn't worry so much, I could:

1. _____

2. _____

3. _____

4. _____

5. _____

4. Investigate your worry

Imagine yourself as Sherlock Holmes with a huge magnifying glass. You are now going to examine your worry.

Interrogate it. Is it rooted in anything real? Does your worry belong more to the realm of fact or fear?

If you are worried about what someone else thinks of you, you are making one of the more common thinking errors of 'mind-reading'. This is an assumption that needs to be challenged.

Write down what you are worrying about and then try to determine whether it is rooted in fact or fear.

_____

_____

_____

_____

If you are worried about your electricity being cut off because you haven't been able to pay the bill, then this worry is rooted in fact and requires action. However, worrying that someone doesn't like you because they didn't acknowledge you the last time you saw them is not rooted in fact, it is rooted in interpretation.

Identify the evidence you think supports this worry's right to exist.

1. _____

2. _____

3. _____

Next, make a list of evidence that doesn't support this worry's right to exist.

1. _____

2. _____

3. _____

The first step to deal with worries that are based on fact is to take control and step back into your own power. Make a list of things you *can* do, steps you *can* take, such as phoning your electricity supplier to come to a payment plan.

Make a list of the supports that are available to you and the people who may be able to help you.

1. _____

2. _____

3. _____

4. _____

5. _____

Discuss your plan with someone close to you who is supportive. If your worries belong to the realm of fiction rather than fact, then Chapter 3 on challenging your thinking will help you to identify your thinking errors and change your thinking patterns of 'catastrophising', mind-reading and magnification that are feeding your worries and keeping them alive.

5. Limit the time you spend worrying

If you find you are spending a lot of time worrying every day, it is important that you take some control back from your worries by limiting the amount of time you devote to them.

Allow yourself a half hour every day to do all your worrying. Choose a particular time to do this when you won't be disturbed. Give yourself permission to do nothing else except worry during this time. It may help to have a notebook with you and write down your worries during this time. Set an alarm for thirty minutes later and when the time is up, make a decision to stop worrying until your dedicated worry time the following day.

If during the rest of the day you begin to worry, say to yourself, 'I am not going to think about that now, I will wait until my worry time.' You may have to remind yourself and 'thought stop' a few times during the day, but gradually you will find yourself worrying less outside of your dedicated time.

6. Avoid avoidance

Worry is disempowering and can cause a cycle of paralysis. The paralysis of worry prevents action and fosters avoidance.

Strange as it may seem, this is the *good* news because now you know that by tackling your pattern of avoidance, you can break the worry cycle. *Is there a task you are avoiding at the moment because of worry? Is there someone you are avoiding because of worry?*

Make a list of the things, people and/or situations that you are avoiding because of your worry. Writing this list is, in itself, an action – and as soon as you start to act, the cycle will be broken and your anxiety will subside because immediately the balance of power shifts from the worry back to you.

1. _____

2. _____

3. _____

4. _____

5. _____

If your worry is rooted in fact, ask yourself what supports you need to help you deal with it. Who can you speak to about it? Where can you get some advice or help? By doing this, your worry becomes a problem that has to be tackled and, very slowly, your relationship with your worry will begin to change.

The change occurs as you begin to take control of what is causing you to worry.

7. Work with your breathing

Worry sucks the breath out of life, contracting the spirit and curling the body in on itself. Ironically, by increasing your awareness of your breathing patterns and making some simple adjustments, you can begin to connect with the energy and the vitality of your own breath.

How can altering your breathing pattern have such an effect on your symptoms of anxiety? Humans tend to use two main styles of breathing: *upper-chest breathing*, which tends to be short, rapid intakes of breath, and *diaphragmatic breathing*, which comes from the abdomen and tends to be much deeper and slower.

Research has shown that when we become anxious, we engage much more in upper-chest breathing and this pattern of hyperventilation, or over-breathing, plays a significant role in increasing our symptoms of anxiety.

From a scientific point of view, this is how it works. Rapid, short breathing increases your intake of oxygen and decreases the level of carbon dioxide in your bloodstream, thus altering the pH level, constricting blood vessels and increasing your heart rate. The increased alkalinity makes the nerve cells more excitable – on red alert to activate the fight or flight response. This is great if you are an athlete running down the back straight in sight of victory – but, if you are not, your rapid shallow pattern of breathing can cause a whole range of very distressing physical symptoms, including dizziness, sweating, light-headedness, shaking, muscle pain, heart palpitations and disorientation. These symptoms appear very rapidly and seem to come from nowhere, creating intense anxiety.

The good news is that once you know what causes something, you have the key to reversing the pattern.

The following is a simple, abdominal breathing exercise that will help you take control of your breathing and slow it down, enabling you to move to a deeper, more relaxed form of breathing and bypassing the anxiety-provoking side-effects of over-breathing. This happens because the oxygen supply to your brain and body, which stimulates the parasympathetic nervous system, is increased, and this promotes a deep sense of calm, which is the opposite to the fight or flight response.

But don't take our word for it – try it out.

Abdominal breathing exercise

To begin with, find a comfortable chair and sit with both feet firmly on the ground. Close your eyes. Place both hands on your chest and take four short, quick intakes of breath. After the fourth intake, place your hands by your side and breathe normally for two breaths.

Next, place your hands on your chest again and begin to move them slowly down from your chest area to rest on your stomach. Pause for a moment and imagine your lungs are located in your stomach area and your hands are resting on them. Take a deep inhalation through your nose, slowly breathing life into your lungs. Take note of the gentle rise of your two hands as they move upwards and outwards with the expansion of your abdomen.

Take at least six slow, deep breaths in this position – each time breathe in for a count of five and breathe out for a count of seven. Each in-out sequence counts as one breath.

Breathe in for a count of five and breathe out for a count of seven. As you breathe out, allow your body to let go of any tension you are holding. Become aware of how you are feeling in your body as you do this exercise.

Take a moment to write down what the experience of doing this exercise was like for you.

_____

_____

Make a plan for the next week. Write down a time for each day when you will set aside five or ten minutes to do this exercise.

	Mon	Tue	Wed	Thurs	Fri	Sat	Sun
Morning							
Evening							

Gradually over time, if you extend the number of abdominal breaths that you take and do this exercise on a daily basis (particularly when you feel anxious), you will notice a greater feeling of well-being and a reduction of your anxious symptoms.

The great thing about this exercise is that you can practise it anywhere. If you are in a coffee shop or on a train and start to feel symptoms of anxiety, you can discreetly shift your breathing to your abdomen, begin the exercise and restore a feeling of calm.

8. Harness the energy of worry

Every professional actor, painter, sculptor and musician worries before a performance or exhibition. When we see them on stage, we say, 'They're effortless.' If they are effortless in their performance, it's because of the effort they've put into their preparation. They have harnessed the energy of their anxiety and used it to enhance their performance and unleash their creative energy.

Just take a moment to imagine how you could use the energy you spend worrying in a more positive, creative way.

_____

_____

_____

9. Practise relaxation

It is almost impossible to be worried and relaxed at the same time. When we are worried or stressed, we tend to tense our muscles and, without even being aware of it, we hold our bodies very tightly. This tension and tightness in our bodies can make us even more worried as we interpret the tension as confirmation of our fears. Learning to release the tension that is held in your body will help you feel more relaxed, less anxious, and will mean you find it easier to make decisions and feel less driven by outside pressures.

The following practice of progressive muscle relaxation will help you relax muscular tension stored in your body and will help reduce symptoms of anxiety if you practise it regularly.

Before you begin the practice, read through the exercise to get a sense of what it is about. Practise this exercise in a quiet place where you are unlikely to be disturbed and try to practise it at the same time each day. Wait at least ninety minutes after you have eaten a meal before beginning the exercise and don't begin if you are feeling hungry. It's also probably best to remove any jewellery, belts and ties and wear loose, comfortable clothes. Remove your shoes and remember to turn off any phones and remove any clocks from the room.

Ideally you should be lying on your back for this exercise but, if you prefer, you can sit in a comfortable chair. Cover yourself with a blanket so that you don't get cold.

Let your arms fall loosely down by the side of your body. Check that your eyes and mouth are gently closed and that you are comfortable. Try to remain still throughout the practice.

Bring your awareness to any sounds outside your body. Sounds that are close by and sounds that are in the distance. Sounds of other people, sounds of animals or traffic. Have awareness of the sounds around you.

Now bring your attention to your body, touching the floor beneath you. Your heels, the back of your legs, your arms, your back, your shoulders, the back of your head. Have awareness of your entire body lying here touching the floor or in contact with the chair.

Now move your focus to your breath. Notice each breath as it slowly enters and leaves your body. Breathing in and breathing out. Breathing in and breathing out. Feel your abdomen rise and fall with each breath that you take. Your body breathing in – your body breathing out.

Bring your attention to the right side of your body. Your right hand. Become aware of your right thumb, your index finger, your long finger, your fourth finger and your little finger. Now, close your right hand into a fist and clench it tightly, clench it tightly as your body breathes in and your body breathes out, your body breathes in and your body breathes out. Slowly allow your right hand to open, open your right hand slowly as you breathe out. Notice the change in your right hand as your muscles become more and more relaxed. Breathing in and out as your muscles become more and more relaxed, more and more relaxed.

Now, bring your attention to your left hand. Become aware of your left thumb, your left index finger, your long finger, your fourth finger and your little finger. Now close your left hand into a fist and clench it tightly, clench it tightly as your body breathes in and your body breathes out, your body breathes in and your body breathes out. Now slowly allow your left hand to open, open your left hand slowly as you breathe out. Notice the change in your left hand as your muscles become more and more relaxed. Breathing in and out as your muscles become more and more relaxed, more and more relaxed.

Next, slowly close both hands into fists and clench both fists together. Clench both fists tightly as your body breathes in and your body breathes out, your body breathes in and your body breathes out. Now, slowly allow both your hands to open, slowly open both your hands as you breathe out. Notice your muscles becoming more and more relaxed. Breathing in and out as your muscles become more and more relaxed, more and more relaxed.

Bring your attention now to your right arm. As you breathe in, slowly bring your hand up to touch your right shoulder, hold it there as you breathe in and out, slowly breathing in and out, breathing in and out. Now, gently allow your hand to return to its resting place. Become aware of the change in your arm as your muscles becomes more and more relaxed, more and more relaxed.

Next, turn your attention to your left arm. As you breathe in, slowly bring your left hand up to touch your left shoulder, hold it there as you breathe in and out, slowly breathing in and out, breathing in and out. Now gently allow your hand to return to its resting place. Become aware of the change in your arm as your muscles becomes more and more relaxed, more and more relaxed.

Now, slowly raise both your arms to your shoulders, hold them there as you breathe in and out, slowly breathing in and out, breathing in and out. Next, gently allow your arms to return to the ground, become aware of the change in your arms as your muscles become more and more relaxed, more and more relaxed.

Bring your attention to your right shoulder. Raise this shoulder up to your right ear. Hold it there, hold it there for a count of three, and then allow it to return to its resting place. Once again, raise this shoulder up to your right ear. Hold it there, hold it there for a count of three, then allow it to return to its resting place. Notice the muscles in your shoulder becoming more and more relaxed and allow that shoulder to relax even further.

Bring your attention to your left shoulder. Raise this shoulder up to your left ear. Hold it there, hold it there for a count of three, then allow it to return to its resting place. Again, raise this shoulder up to your left ear. Hold it there, hold it there, then allow it to return to its resting place. Notice the muscles in your shoulder becoming more and more relaxed and allow that shoulder to relax even further.

Now, raise both shoulders together. Hold them for a count of three, and then allow them to return to their resting place. Once again, raise both shoulders together. Hold them for three and then allow them to return to their resting place.

Now, bring your awareness to your stomach. Take a deep breath in and, as you do, tighten the muscles of your stomach. Hold the muscles in, hold them in, hold them in. Now breathe out slowly and, as you do, release them further and further and notice the change as your stomach muscles become more and more relaxed, allow them to become more and more relaxed.

Next, bring your attention to your buttocks. Clench your right buttock tightly as you breathe in, hold it in tightly, hold it tightly, then slowly release it to its resting position as you breathe out. Notice the difference in your buttock as it becomes more and more relaxed, more and more relaxed. Now, bring your attention to your left buttock lying on the ground. Clench your left buttock tightly as you breathe in, hold it in tightly, hold it tightly, then slowly release it to its resting position as you breathe out. Notice the difference in your buttock as it becomes more and more relaxed, more and more relaxed. Now squeeze both buttocks together as you breathe in, holding in, holding in. Now slowly breathe out as you release them back to their resting place. Notice the difference as they become more and more relaxed, more and more relaxed.

Next, bring your attention to your thighs lying on the ground. Squeeze your right thigh in tightly as you breathe in, hold it in tightly, hold it tightly then slowly release it to its resting position as you breathe out. Notice the difference in your right thigh as it becomes more and more relaxed, more and more relaxed. Now, bring your attention to your left thigh lying on the ground. Squeeze your left thigh in tightly as you breathe in, hold it in tightly, hold it tightly, then slowly release it to its resting position as you breathe out. Notice the difference in your thigh as it becomes more and more relaxed, more and more relaxed. Now, squeeze both thighs together as you breathe in, holding in, holding in, then slowly breathe out as you release them back to their resting place. Notice the difference as they become more and more relaxed, more and more relaxed.

Next, bring your attention to your calves. Squeeze your right calf in tightly as you breathe in, hold it in tightly, hold it tightly, then slowly release it to its resting position as you breathe out. Notice the difference in your right calf as it becomes more and more relaxed, more and more relaxed. Now, bring your attention to your left calf. Squeeze your left calf in tightly as you breathe in, hold it in tightly, hold it tightly, then slowly release it to its resting position as you breathe out. Notice the difference in your calf as it becomes more and more relaxed, more and more relaxed. Now, squeeze both calves together as you breathe in, holding in, holding in, now slowly breathe out as you release them back to their resting place. Notice the difference as they become more and more relaxed, more and more relaxed.

Next, bring your attention to your feet. Curl your right foot in tightly as you breathe in, hold it in tightly, hold it tightly, then slowly release it to its resting position as you breathe out. Notice the difference in your right foot as it becomes more and more relaxed, more and more relaxed. Now, bring your attention to your left foot. Curl your left foot in tightly as you breathe in, hold it in tightly, hold it tightly, then slowly release it to its resting position as you breathe out. Notice the difference in your foot as it becomes more and more relaxed, more and more relaxed. Next, curl both feet together as you breathe in, holding in, holding in, now slowly breathe out as you release them back to their resting place. Notice the difference as they become more and more relaxed, more and more relaxed.

Next, move your attention to your face. Pull your eyebrows in together as you breathe in, hold them together, hold them together, then gently release them as you breathe out. Notice the change in your forehead as it releases the tension and becomes more and more relaxed, more and more relaxed. Once more, pull you eyebrows in together as you breathe in, hold them together, hold them together, now gently release them as you breathe out. Notice the change in your forehead as it releases the tension and becomes more and more relaxed, more and more relaxed.

As you breathe in, close your eyes tightly, hold them closed, hold them closed, then, as you breathe out gently, release them and allow your eyelids to droop. Notice your eyes becoming more and more relaxed as they let the tension go and become more and more relaxed. Once more, as you breathe in, close your eyes tightly, hold them closed, hold them closed, then, as you breathe out, gently release them and allow your eyelids to droop. Notice your eyes becoming more and more relaxed as they let the tension go and sink deeper and deeper.

Now, bring your attention to your nose. Wrinkle up your nose as you breathe in, hold it, hold it, then, as you breathe out, allow your nose to relax. Notice the release of tension in your nose as it becomes more and more relaxed. Once more, bring your attention to your nose. Wrinkle up your nose as you breathe in, hold it, hold it, then, as you breathe out, allow your nose to relax. Notice the release of tension in your nose as it becomes more and more relaxed.

Bring your attention to your jaw. Clench your back teeth together as you breathe in and hold it, hold it, then, as you breathe out, release the tension in your jaw and notice the difference as the muscles in your jaw become more and more relaxed, more and more relaxed. Once more, bring your attention to your jaw. Clench your back teeth together as you breathe in, hold it, hold it, then, as you breathe out, release the tension in your jaw and notice the difference as the muscles in your jaw become more and more relaxed, more and more relaxed.

Now, become aware of your whole body from your head to your toes – have awareness of your whole body. Now, connect with the sensation of heaviness in your body. Feel that your arms are heavy, your legs are heavy, your upper body is heavy, your lower body feels heavy. Feel this sensation of heaviness in your whole body as if you are sinking deeper and deeper into the floor or chair.

Allow your body to relax further and further, deeper and deeper into the floor or into the chair.

Now, imagine that you are lying on a soft grassy bank by a river. It is a warm summer's day. You are lying on your back and you feel a cool gentle breeze on your face. Nearby you can hear the soothing sounds of the river as it flows by. As you gaze at the clear, blue sky, you feel more and more relaxed and at peace with yourself. Breathing in, breathing out, fully relaxed and at peace ... Breathing in, breathing out, deeply relaxed and at peace ... breathing in, breathing out. After a long while, you realise that it is time to leave this place and very slowly you get up and begin to walk back up the hill to return home. As you approach the top of the hill, you look back down to the peaceful spot where you were lying and you know that you can return to this special place any time you wish.

Next, slowly move your attention back to your breathing – your body breathing. Your stomach gently rising with each breath that you breathe, your breath moving in and out of your body. Now, take a long, deep breath in and feel that you are breathing peace and contentment into your body and, as you breathe out, feel that you are letting go of all tension and stress.

Bring your awareness to your body as it rests – the contact your body has with the floor, all the sounds around you. The sounds within the room, the sounds in the distance. Be aware of how you feel right now.

Slowly start moving your body, your hands, your feet, gently moving your body from side to side. Slowly open your eyes and come back into the room.

The practice has now ended.

After the practice, be aware of how you are feeling in your body and make a note of this in your journal.

The energy and time you reclaim from worrying will be available for you to use in all kinds of creative, positive ways in your life. In the next two chapters, we will show you how engaging in meditation, and a regular exercise routine will also help you to reduce your anxiety and improve your sense of well-being.

Pathway Eight

Explore Meditation

When did 'busy' become a virtue? When did we adopt the motto: 'I *do*, therefore I am?' Constant activity can give the illusion of achievement. We are tempted to fill the hours and yet 'haven't a minute'.

A few years ago, I was invited to a Buddhist temple in upstate New York to film the monks meditating. I was startled to see huge drums assembled to the side of the main hall. We had no sooner lowered ourselves onto the hard stools than a Buddhist nun attacked the drums with blurring sticks. The booming vibrated through the soles of my feet and shivered through my body until my teeth seemed to rattle. Suddenly, it was over. The profound silence that followed was emphasised by the faint rustle of cloth and the slight creak of stools as the monks settled to meditate. I wondered if the drumming was intended to drive distracting thoughts from our minds or to shake the tensions from our bodies and leave us calm and receptive.

Beside me, the abbot sat, as if carved from stone – although stone is too rigid a word to describe his calm.

For the next hour, I smelled incense, heard birdsong from outside and felt the seat harden beneath me. My mind bubbled with questions. Should I be chanting some mantra to bring me peace? Should I regulate my breathing? Would some deep revelation come if I tried harder? Finally, I drew a deep breath down to the pit of my stomach and let all those sensations and thoughts fly like balloons as I breathed out. And, for a time – too short a time – I felt the deep inner peace of simply being.

Meditation is a very ancient art that has been practised for thousands of years. It involves the slowing down and stilling of the mind to create a deeper state of awareness, one that is without thinking or doing. When practised regularly over a period of time, it can be deeply nourishing. It has the power to still the troubled seas of the mind and to help you cultivate a deeper connection with your own compassion, wisdom and self-acceptance. It is very effective in helping to treat symptoms of anxiety, depression and stress. You can meditate anywhere – in the privacy of your own home, at your desk at lunch-time or on the bus – and it costs nothing to do. It is a powerful resource that is freely available and it will enhance your sense of well-being if you practise it regularly.

When you are beginning to meditate, it is important that you do so for short periods of time, beginning with five- to ten-minute sessions. In this chapter, there are four different meditations for you to try.

The first is a short introductory breathing meditation that focuses on your breathing, helping to relax your body and calm your mind. If you haven't meditated before, we recommend that you begin with this practice. When you are comfortable with this meditation, you can move on to the other meditation practices, which are longer.

The second meditation focuses on connecting you with the flow and experience of your own vitality. The third is best done after you have read Chapter 4, 'Talk Back to Negative Self-Talk'. The final meditation is one that helps you to connect with your own 'inner teacher' in a way that can be very healing and nourishing. When you complete a meditation, it's a good idea to make a note in your journal of what the experience was like for you. Read each meditation through once or twice so that you are familiar with it before you start.

Meditation one – Breathing meditation (five to ten minutes)

Start by finding a place of stillness where you can sit comfortably and where you won't be disturbed for ten minutes. Remember to turn off phones, computers and anything that might intrude on your space as you meditate. Sit into the chair, place your legs firmly on the floor and allow yourself to get comfortable. Place a hand on each thigh with your palms facing up, allowing your thumb to touch the tip of your index finger on each hand.

When you are ready to start, gently close your eyes and go inside yourself, leaving behind the distractions of the outside world. (If you find it difficult to close your eyes, allow your focus to soften and half-close them.)

Bring your awareness to your breathing – to the ebb and flow of your breath as it enters and leaves your body. Just observe your breathing without changing it, gradually allowing your breath to deepen until it seems to come from a space below your navel. Breathe deeply into this space. Become aware of your breath as it enters your body, travels slowly down the back of your throat and into your lungs. Become aware of your lungs gently expanding and moving out and up. Notice your breath as it begins to leave your lungs and to travel up and out through your mouth. Breathe gently and with awareness.

As you breathe, practise the following technique. Breathe in slowly through your nose for a count of four. Hold your breath for two seconds and then breathe out slowly for a count of six. Inhale for one ... two ... three ... four. Hold for one ... two. Exhale through your mouth for one ... two ... three ... four ... five ... six.

If you notice any tension in your body, bring your attention to that area and, with each deep breath, allow your body to become more relaxed. With each in-breath, breathe in a sense of deep calm and peace, and with each out-breath, imagine that you are letting go of any tension. Practise this breath-counting technique for about five minutes.

When you feel ready, slowly bring your attention back to the room you are in. Become aware of the sounds around you. Become aware of your body sitting in the chair. When you are ready, gently open your eyes and take a moment to allow yourself to come back into the room and become accustomed to the sights and sounds around you.

Take a moment to make a note of what this experience was like for you and note any feelings you have.

You can do this meditation at any time. Repeat it every day for five days and note how you are feeling after each meditation.

Meditation two – Vitality meditation (fifteen to twenty minutes)

Start by finding a place of stillness where you can sit comfortably and where you won't be disturbed for twenty minutes. Remember to turn off phones, computers and anything that might intrude on your space as you meditate.

When you are ready to start, gently close your eyes and go inside yourself. (If you find it difficult to close your eyes, allow your focus to soften and half-close them.)

Bring your awareness to your breathing and become aware of the ebb and flow of your breath as it enters and leaves your body. Just observe your breathing without changing it, gradually allowing your breath to deepen until it seems to come from a space below your navel. Breathe deeply into this space for four or five breaths.

If you notice any tension in your body, bring your attention to that area and with each deep breath allow your body to become more relaxed – with each in-breath, feel you are breathing in a sense of calm and peace and with each out-breath, feel you are letting go of any tension.

From this quiet space within yourself, remember a time in your life when you felt really connected with your own vitality. This memory can be from any age or any time in your life. It can be a memory you shared with someone else or of a time when you were alone. It can be a memory that lasted a long time or an experience that was just a fleeting moment.

Describe the scene to yourself silently. Recall where you were, and who you were with. Remember the sounds, the smells and the feeling of vitality that made you choose this memory from all the memories you could have chosen. Allow yourself to breathe deeply into this connection with yourself.

Are there one or two words that capture the essence of this experience for you? If so, you may wish to say the first word silently on the in-breath and say the second word on the out-breath. Say the first word silently on the in-breath and say the second word silently on the out-breath.

With each in-breath, feel the warm energy flow into and circulate around your body, extending to your fingertips and down to your toes.

Allow yourself to breathe into and savour this experience for about ten minutes. Then slowly bring your attention back to the room you are in. Become aware of the sounds around you. Become aware of your body sitting in the chair. When you are ready, gently open your eyes and take a moment to allow yourself to come back into the room and become accustomed to the sights and sounds around you.

Take a moment to make a note in your journal of what this experience was like for you and of feelings that you have.

You can do this meditation at any time. Repeat it every day for five days and note how you are feeling after each meditation.

When I practise this meditation, I always feel renewed and revitalised. For me, the memory that came to me the first time I practised it was from a time when I was thirteen years old and on a school trip to the west of Ireland. About mid-afternoon when we were making our way home, the tour bus broke down and we were delayed for a couple of hours. I remember a small group of us went into the fields behind where the bus broke down and climbed to the top of a small hill. The views of the surrounding countryside were spectacular. We lay down in the grass, gazing up at the sky. I remember the heat of the sun beating down on me, and the feel of the grass. I remember the sound of the crickets in the grass, the bees buzzing happily and the intoxicating honey-sweet smell of the gorse bushes. I could feel the heat rising up as if the earth was breathing out and, for those few moments, I felt fully alive and deeply connected to all that was living around me. When I return to this experience during times of meditation, I find it deeply nourishing.

Meditation three – Positive affirmations meditation (ten to fifteen minutes)

If you practise it regularly, this meditation will work to promote a more positive self-image and help rebuild and strengthen your self-esteem.

To do this meditation you will need to have completed the affirmations exercises in Chapter 4. In that chapter you compiled a list of fifteen positive self-statements that you believe about yourself. Remember to re-check your list of affirmations before you begin this meditation to make sure they: begin with 'I', are short, simple statements that you can really own, are positive and contain no negatives, and are in the present tense. Before beginning the meditation, select three affirmations from your list of fifteen.

Start by finding a place of stillness where you can sit comfortably and where you won't be disturbed for fifteen minutes. Remember to turn off phones, computers and anything that might intrude on your space as you meditate.

When you are ready, gently close your eyes and bring your awareness to your breathing. (If you find it difficult to close your eyes, allow your focus to soften and half-close them.)

Become aware of the ebb and flow of your breath as it enters and leaves your body. Just observe your breathing without changing it, gradually allow your breath to deepen until it seems to come from a space below your navel. If, at any time, you find yourself becoming distracted by thoughts, just bring your awareness back to the rhythm of your breathing.

Breathe deeply and slowly into this space for four or five breaths. If you notice any tension in your body, bring your attention to that area and with each deep breath allow your body to become more relaxed. With each in-breath, feel a sense of calm and peace entering your body and with each out-breath, feel that you are letting go of any tension.

At this moment of deep relaxation, gently recall the three positive affirmations you selected. Repeat each one of them three times, silently to yourself and in tune with the rhythm of your breathing. As you say each affirmation, slowly and gently, allow yourself to fully receive it. Imagine it rippling out and filling your whole body with warmth and nourishment. When you have repeated each affirmation to yourself three times, allow yourself to sit for a while in this deep connection with your true self. Receive any feelings you may have.

When you feel ready, slowly bring your attention back to the room you are in. Become aware of the sounds around you. Become aware of your body sitting in the chair. When you are ready, gently open your eyes and take a moment to allow yourself to come back into the room and become accustomed to the sights and sounds around you.

Take a moment to make a note of what this experience was like for you and any feelings you have.

You can do this meditation at any time. Repeat the meditation every day for five days and note how you feel after each meditation. You can choose to select a different set of three affirmations for each meditation.

Meditation four – Inner-teacher meditation (fifteen to twenty minutes)

The inner-teacher meditation is a meditative practice that enables you to open up a deep connection to the wisdom and support of your inner teacher – who, for example, could be someone from your own history, perhaps a teacher or grandparent or friend whose guidance and wisdom has been very influential in your life and a source of strength and nourishment for you in the past. Your inner teacher could also be something symbolic that has meaning for you. It could be an animal or bird or, indeed, it could be some aspect of yourself. In the meditation, you will bring any problem or question that is troubling you in your life at the moment to your inner teacher.

Start by finding a place of stillness where you can sit comfortably and where you won't be disturbed for the next twenty minutes.

Remember to turn off all phones, computers or anything that might intrude on your space while you meditate. Sit in your chair, place your legs firmly on the floor and allow yourself to get comfortable. Place a hand on each thigh with your palms facing up, enabling your thumb to touch the tip of your index finger in each hand.

When you are ready to start, gently close your eyes and go inside yourself. (If you find it difficult to close your eyes, allow your focus to soften and half-close them.)

Bring your awareness to your body as you sit here on the chair. Become aware of the contact you have with the floor and with the chair. Now bring your awareness to your breathing. Become aware of the ebb and flow of your breath as it enters and leaves your body. Just observe your breathing without changing it. Gradually allow your breathing to deepen until it seems to come from a space below your navel. If you find yourself becoming distracted by thoughts at any time, just bring your awareness back to the rhythm of your breathing.

Breathe deeply into this space below your navel for four or five breaths, simply following the movement of your breath as it gently enters and leaves your body. Now imagine that you are walking down a country lane with fields on either side. As you pass by, you see cattle grazing in the field. There is a gentle breeze blowing and you feel very peaceful as you walk. After a few minutes' walking, you see a wooden gate to the left. You decide to go through the gate and follow the small path that leads into an oak wood. As you walk through the wood, you feel warmed by the gentle breeze rustling through the trees. You walk deeper into the woods and, after a while, you see a clearing ahead. As you approach the clearing, you see a small log cabin with smoke rising from the chimney. You notice that the door of the cabin is open invitingly.

You pause for a minute at the threshold before entering. As you walk into the cabin, you see your inner teacher sitting by the fire, looking towards you and smiling warmly. You sit in the chair opposite and rest in the gentle silence that is between you. After a while, you experience a sense of being completely accepted and understood ...

At this moment of deep connection with your inner teacher, you describe what is troubling you – if you have a question, you can ask it now. Wait in the silence and receive the answer that emerges in whatever form it takes. You stay for a little while longer and then, when you are ready, you say goodbye to and thank your inner teacher. You walk through the door and back towards the woods. As you leave, you pause for a moment and look back over your shoulder at the little cabin, knowing that you are welcome to return to this place at any time.

You move back through the woods and down the path that leads to the wooden gate. As you close the gate behind you and walk closer to home, you feel a deep sense of contentment and peace.

Now bring your attention back to your breathing, following the inhalation and exhalation without changing it. Become aware of the sounds around you and of your body sitting in the chair. The meditation is now over. Begin to move from side to side in the chair and, when you are ready, gently open your eyes.

Take a few moments to write about what you experienced in your journal and identify any feelings you are aware of at the end of the meditation.

Pathway Nine

Embrace Exercise

At weekends, my dad often walked my brother and me to Ross's Wood which was about a five-mile hike from our home. It was a long walk for short legs but I don't remember either of us complaining. As far as we were concerned, we were out with our dad and every field and furze held the promise of rabbits and birds' nests. We took a meandering route, like the stream that dawdled through the valley.

We were exercising without knowing it. The walking stimulated our limbs, lungs and hearts but we didn't realise that our spirits and our relationships were also getting a workout.

It might sound stunningly obvious to say, but we depend heavily on our bodies to help us get through the cut and thrust of our daily living. Just think about what you ask your body to do on a daily basis – run up and down stairs, travel to work or school, walk endlessly, lift, clean, shop, push buggies, cook meals, iron, wash, eat, drink, absorb, digest, eliminate. We demand so much from our bodies, yet very often we overlook the fact that our bodies have a limited amount of energy and we neglect to take good care of our own physical well-being. When we are tired and exhausted in our bodies, it affects our mood and this, in turn, affects how we think about and relate to ourselves, the world and others. The choices and options available to us become more limited.

As part of your overall plan to enhance the quality of your life and well-being, it is important to take some time to look at your relationship with your body and to explore how you can develop ways to take greater care of your own physical health.

How do you relate to your body?

Take some time to consider how you would describe your relationship with your body. Do you take care of your body or do you take it for granted? Do you make a lot of demands on your body? Is it a positive, healthy relationship, or is it a relationship characterised by abuse and neglect?

_____

_____

_____

_____

_____

If your body could talk, what would it say about the relationship?

_____

_____

_____

_____

What would your body like you to stop doing?

_____

_____

_____

_____

_____

What would your body like you to start doing?

_____

_____

_____

_____

_____

Name three things that you really like about your body.

1. _____

2. _____

3. _____

Now ask yourself the following question:

What does my body need *from me to enable it to help me with my goal of leading a fuller and happier life?*

_____

_____

_____

_____

_____

_____

_____

_____

_____

What are the steps you can take to support your body to meet its needs?

_____

_____

_____

_____

_____

_____

_____

Exercising

Regular exercise can play an important part in nurturing your body and helping you to lead a more balanced and fulfilling life. Studies show that people who exercise regularly receive a whole range of physical, psychological and social benefits. A regular programme of just three hours' exercise a week spread over five sessions has been shown to have a huge range of benefits, including enhanced feelings of well-being, improved concentration, self-esteem and increased fitness. It can also reduce symptoms of depression through the release of endorphins which create a greater sense of well-being. When you exercise, your body takes in more oxygen and this increased oxygenation of the blood and brain improves alertness, concentration and accuracy. Exercise also helps reduce vulnerability to panic attacks by reducing muscle tension, discharging built-up frustration and facilitating the processing of excess adrenalin and thyroxin in the bloodstream that builds up when your body's natural fight or flight reaction is triggered.

Other physical benefits include a lowering of cholesterol levels and blood pressure, better circulation, improved digestion, and increased energy levels. It can help you lose weight, tone up and look healthy. In turn, all this affects how you feel about yourself.

Exercise can also have a range of social benefits because it encourages you to go out more, and if you exercise with other people as part of a team or class, it can increase your social contact and social support. The good news is that these benefits begin to take effect within a very short space of time. Overall, as one of our sons would say, it is a 'no brainer', a win-win situation – so what stops you from getting involved?

Take a moment to describe your relationship with exercise. When the word is mentioned, do you feel a moan coming on that travels down to your boots, or do you feel a sense of excitement and curiosity? Is it something you think you might enjoy taking up or are you dreading the prospect?

When the word 'exercise' is mentioned, I _____

_____

_____

_____

_____

What is your current position with regard to exercise? Would you say at the moment that you exercise:

Never _____ *Rarely* _____ *Occasionally* ____ *Regularly* _____?

Do you think that your overall quality of life would benefit from receiving the range of physical, psychological and social benefits which come with participation in a regular exercise programme?

Yes ___ *No* ___

If the answer is yes, then list the specific ways in which you feel you would benefit if you exercised regularly. When answering this question, consider the impact on your body, your health, your mood, your overall well-being, self-esteem and your relationships with others.

If I took exercise on a regular basis, I _____

_____

_____

_____

_____

_____

Have you ever started an exercise programme or class in the past? If so, describe the programme – what worked? Why did you begin the programme? Was there anything you enjoyed about it?

_____

_____

_____

_____

_____

Now consider what interrupted you – what stopped you continuing your exercise programme?

_____

_____

_____

_____

From your experience, what do you know about which type of exercise programme works for you? Do you work better alone or would participating in an exercise class make it more likely for you to achieve your goal?

_____

_____

_____

_____

_____

_____

When it comes to planning the right exercise programme for you, there is a whole range of options to choose from. Some are solitary, some are group-based. Below are some options, you may think of some others.

- An individual walking programme
- A joint walking programme with a friend
- Joining a hill-walking group
- Jogging alone or with a friend
- Running
- Swimming
- Cycling
- Joining a soccer club
- Playing rugby or tag rugby
- Rowing
- Ballroom Dancing
- Sailing
- Badminton
- Gardening
- Martial arts
- Bowling
- Golf

- Tennis
- Joining a gym
- Zumba dance classes
- Yoga classes
- Belly dancing
- Climbing
- Archery
- Volleyball
- Canoeing/Kayaking
- Surfing
- Gymnastics
- Other

Have some fun

When you are choosing an exercise programme, try to connect with your playful side. Exercise doesn't have to be a chore and you don't have to take yourself too seriously. It can be fun if you allow yourself to engage with it playfully and remain open to possibilities. Ask yourself what you would really love to do if you didn't hold yourself back.

Does anything from the list above strike you as being really fun to try? If you can choose something that you might enjoy, you are much more likely to stick with it. If, as well as improving your fitness level, your exercise programme also helps you to meet some of your social goals, this may make it easier to commit to it at times when your motivation dips.

If you have concerns about your health or have never exercised and are overweight, you should consult your doctor for a physical check-up before you start any exercise programme.

Planning to succeed with your exercise programme

Your goal of increasing your level of exercise and becoming fitter is more likely to succeed if you do the following:

- Start slowly and build up your programme gradually. Don't

set yourself up for failure by trying to move from taking no exercise at all to a half-hour run in a week.

- Draw up a specific plan and place the plan somewhere you will see it every day.
- Identify regular times and days when you will exercise. Pick times and days that take into account any demands of work or home, and choose the times that you are most likely to commit to on an ongoing basis.
- Describe what exercise you will take.
- Plan how long the sessions will last.
- Identify where you will exercise. If you are planning to walk or run, pick a location that is pleasant.
- Anticipate things that might interrupt your plan (e.g. birthdays or visitors) and build in a way of dealing with them.
- Identify whom you will exercise with, if you are planning to exercise with a group or friend. Have a back-up plan if this person becomes unavailable.
- Record when you do exercise and make a note in your journal of how you feel after each session. This will help maintain your motivation.
- Watch out for the 'all or nothing' thinking error. If you miss one day's exercise, it doesn't mean the whole plan has failed. Review what got in the way of your plan and plan your next exercise session.
- Share your plan with someone close to you who is supportive.
- Reward and celebrate your achievements. Try to pick rewards that increase your motivation and don't undermine your exercise programme. For example, try to avoid food- or alcohol-based rewards.

Becoming part of a sporting club or organisation is another way to develop a regular exercise programme, and this can also help you meet people and become more involved in your community. Team sports can play a very important role in the lives of children, as Christy's poem 'The Disciple' celebrates.

I too was reared
A Sunday pilgrim to the Park.
I knew the smell of jersey-sweat,
The sap of orange,
Running from the fingers of the hand-root
Down the grain of banded ash.
I too could glean the shattered hurley
Running rescued from the fray.
One heady day
With patience of a printing monk
I burned 'Excalibur' upon the shaft.
And though I too could pick it clean,
Could hit it right or left,
Could bow beneath the swing
To block, push,
Scourge it with the best of them,
A part of me knew sure and all the time
That I would never
Christy Ring-a-rosy round bewildered backs
To shake the net
And ripple roars
Across the Sunday Park.
I fought it with an extra lap,
An hour alone at coursing, lifting,
Striking sodden leather
Or risking shin where hurley should have been,

Notching up the white-scar Ogham
Crisscross written on the bone.
Dreading the late-flung orange at half-time,
Name uncalled and pep-talk just begun.
And yet, I don't begrudge their glory
Hard wrought in the sweat of summer evenings.
They planed my boy-edge smooth with dedication,
Gave me Saints and Heroes I could worship,
Wove me dreams to warm my winter evenings.

Can you identify with any of the experiences described in the poem?
Make a note of any thoughts, memories or feelings you are aware of.

_____

_____

_____

_____

Unfortunately, as we get older we tend to drift away from this kind of involvement and become spectators rather than participants. There are team sports and exercise groups for all ages in almost every community. Why not check out what the options are near you?

Pathway Ten

Face Your Anger

I unleashed my anger,
and the world trembled.
White hot words erupted from my mouth.
My rage consumed my heart,
Blinding my eyes to feelings,
Dulling my ears to fears.

I swallowed my anger and my soul sickened,
The unsaid soured and distilled,
Curdling my heart until my heart corroded
And scalded those I loved with acid words.

I spoke my hurt
Wrapped in calm words and even tone,
No sharp-edged bitter words
To bare the marrow, poison up the bone.
I spoke my hurt and eased my soul
When heart and hurt were heard.

Anger is what we feel when someone, or something, threatens our security or sense of ourselves. It is an essential tool in our human survival kit. Yet, as an emotion, anger gets a lot of bad press – if someone is described as an 'angry person', it is not considered a compliment. However, there is a difference between being angry and being an angry person, and the difference is that most people visit anger but some people actually live there.

We can all use our anger as an instrument to challenge and improve our relationships and society; however, a person possessed by anger *is* the instrument. Their anger is all-consuming to the point that they have no energy left for anything or anyone else. They are weapons in search of a target ... and they're rarely fussy, becoming – to borrow a phrase from Scripture – 'like a roaring lion, going about seeking whom he may devour'.

There are times when, individually and as a society, we need our sense of anger and outrage as a protection and motivation. Anger is the cry of the conscience in the face of injustice, the steam that rises from the oppressed or compressed spirit, the energy that turns the wheel of history. It also has a shadow-side fuelled by disappointment, envy and greed. The fire of unreflected and uncontrolled anger has the capacity to destroy lives and relationships.

In this chapter we will:

- take a close look at the nature of anger
- outline a ten-step approach to help you understand and deal with your anger
- look at ways to resolve, or let go of, old angers
- help you reconnect with your passionate self.

How we learn anger

Anger ferments when our voice is silenced and our needs are

suppressed. This process of suppression and silencing can begin at an early age.

Ask yourself, what words did your parents use about anger – bold, bad, saucy, cheeky? Of course, these words weren't just used to describe the emotion or the angry behaviour, they were used to describe us – 'You are a bold child', 'You are a bad girl.' My personal favourite was 'pup'. It's a word designed to give you a good push and the double-P sounds are sure to soak you. What were the actions that followed the words, apart from a skin graft taken from your rear end? The most memorable and interesting action was the one that sent you to your room.

'Get up those stairs and come down when you have a civil tongue in your head.'

We stamped up the stairs, muttering stuff that would have got us killed downstairs. If there was a mirror on our wardrobe, we 'threw shapes' before it, acting out all the things we should have said. Then, we smelled our dinner and we made the humble pilgrimage downstairs. Principle is noble, but hunger is irresistible.

'Oh, here's the bright boy now. Say you're sorry.'

'I'm sorry.'

'I can't hear you.'

'I'M SORRY.'

'Get up those stairs, you pup.'

There's an official word for this type of punishment – excommunication. Once upon a time, apart from burning at the stake, it was the punishment most people feared. Someone who was excommunicated was put 'outside the tribe' and this punishment is devastating for children – they need to be attached. They become frightened when the contact is broken (hence the insatiable thirst for glasses of water after bedtime). Children who are punished with isolation for being angry learn to hide their anger. They get the message loud and clear that anger is a bad thing, that it is the opposite of good and nice, and that it will lead to exclusion not only from their parents' company but from their parents' love.

So many children are fitted with masks at a young age. They are taught a new vocabulary for surviving anger and to cover it with 'niceness'. People like a child who is nice, is the message that is given. 'Don't talk up' and 'don't talk back' are the instructions. And in case the message isn't clear enough, children are told not to raise their voices in anger – 'Who do you think you're talking to?' is a common remark.

These are the put-downs. Translated, they mean, 'I can yell at you because I'm an adult and you daren't yell at me because you're a child.' This form of bullying has existed in every age. There's a bottomless box of power games, full of masks that can be doled out by the powerful to be worn by the powerless. Once the box is opened, we'll all 'learn, and then know, our place' and we never 'get above ourselves'.

Dysfunctional anger

Do adults ever feel offended, discriminated against, lied to or manipulated? Of course they do. But they have choices. They can use their anger to stand up for themselves and challenge another's behaviour. They can name their hurt and ask for a change, or they can become either 'nice' or 'self-sacrificing'.

Nice people are those who have swallowed the 'nice child' spin. They've learned, hard and early, how to be appreciated in a society that denies the right to be angry. Practise it often enough and long enough, and being nice becomes second nature.

Nice people claim they never feel anger.

But how can anyone live in a world of racism, ageism, sexism and all the other isms and not feel angry? Are they really saying that they don't care enough about anyone or anything to get really angry?

Their mantra is 'let it pass' or 'peace at any price'. But some things are too important to let pass. We don't have to take on everything, but when something or someone who really matters to us is involved, then we really can't 'let it pass'. We only genuinely fight with someone who genuinely matters to us.

Phrases like 'that's his way' or 'that's her age' are unhelpful because they avoid the issue. In the first instance, anyone can and should be challenged to change their 'way', if that way is negative or destructive. Not challenging this type of behaviour is often a form of neglect. Challenge is what keeps people from complacency – and the greatest danger to any relationship is not a 'bust up', but the breakdown that comes from an 'I couldn't be bothered' attitude.

As for 'peace at any price', some prices are just too high, and what passes for peace in those circumstances is really only a ceasefire. Nice people mask their anger but, while the mask keeps them in, it also keeps everyone else out. If our masks are so tight that nothing gets through to us, then that nothing includes love. There's a price to be paid for being human, a cost involved in having a heart and being vulnerable. And it is through our vulnerability that we make real contact with others.

People who give too much

Is it possible to give too much? Surely we should give all we are able to give to those we love? But apart from the fact that too much giving can disable the receiver and create a dependency, there is a very real danger of neglecting the self. We cannot give what we do not have. Those who give too much give up all their rights to their own needs. We may smile at the classic joke about how many self-sacrificing mammies it takes to change a light bulb – answer, none, 'No, I'm grand, love. I'll just sit here in the dark' – but there is a darker side to this. People are often tempted to live for others. In many cultures, self-neglect is raised to the status of a virtue. The downside, of course, is that this person's needs are rarely met, because they never ask for them to be considered.

Those who self-sacrifice have opted for total dedication to others.

However, we are not designed to be totally dedicated to others. The cost of giving in this way is a life spent largely dissatisfied and unfulfilled. Balancing others' needs with our own is essential if we are to be healthy.

People who self-sacrifice are essentially non-assertive, and non-assertiveness can get confused with humility. Humility is not the denial of your own needs but the acceptance of them. Such people also find it difficult to fight fair. While an assertive person would say no to unreasonable requests and take time for themselves, the self-sacrificing person makes themselves totally available to others and neglects themselves. This can lead to resentment of others and low self-esteem. Resentment, by definition, is an anger we feel over and over again but never express or process. It can distil into sarcasm.

Sarcasm is the sour cream of anger – something that has never seen the light of day and has curdled in the shadows. Swallowed anger turns into acid and begins to eat the person from the inside out.

When either of us work with groups on anger, we have lots of laughs and share many stories, but when we get to sarcasm, the laughs become more brittle and the stories become darker. Many people talk about the sarcasm that reduced them to tears as schoolchildren or of a comment about their appearance, family or social circumstances that scalded their young, impressionable psyches and left them scarred. During one recent group session, John told of how he had been reduced to tears as his teacher spoke hurtfully of his family background. Susan related how her sewing had been ridiculed and how she had felt shamed and belittled before her classmates.

Children don't have the vocabulary to respond to sarcasm. 'Sticks and stones will break my bones but names will never hurt me.' Anyone who has suffered as a result of sarcasm knows that this is a nonsense rhyme. A bone will heal, in time, and may even be stronger than it was, but sarcasm can leave an open wound forever.

Important things to know about anger

1. Anger is an important human emotion that we need for our survival. It can be protective and empowering. When channelled in a positive way, it can be a powerful impetus for social change.

2. Anger has a dark side. Uncontrolled anger has the power to damage people, including the person who carries it. If it is left unprocessed, anger can crush the human spirit and disconnect us from our capacity to feel joy and love.

3. Uncontrolled or vengeful anger is called aggression – it is not something we are born with or inherit; it is something we learn. The good news is that what is learned can be unlearned and there are a number of strategies and skills that, if applied consistently, can teach us how to use our anger positively.

4. How we think can play an important role in our anger. In Chapter 3 we looked at the strong connection between thoughts, feelings and actions and the errors that can become part of our way of thinking. How we think affects how we feel and how we behave. Often, it's not what's said or done that gives rise to our anger, but how we interpret what we have heard, seen and experienced; the meaning we perceive in others' actions.

   For example, a neighbour you know well walks right by you in the supermarket without saying hello or giving any acknowledgement. You are surprised and immediately think, *She is ignoring me. She is treating me disrespectfully*. Those thoughts affect your feelings directly. Because you believe you have been ignored or snubbed, you feel angry, disappointed and insulted. Your anger heats up and turns to outrage as it rises to defend your feelings of being slighted. You begin to think of all the things you have done for your neighbour, and all the names you would like to use as you plan ways to return the insult. These feelings act as an internal confirmation that your initial thoughts and interpretations were facts – not just thoughts. This, in turn, makes it more likely that next time you meet your neighbour, you're ready to act on your angry feelings and 'get your own back' – you will, as a famous football manager once advised his players, 'get your retaliation in first'.

But what if you had interpreted the situation differently?

Imagine the same scenario: your neighbour walks right by you at the supermarket and doesn't acknowledge you. However, this time, you think, *She didn't see me* or *She must be very preoccupied or stressed.* Because you're thinking this way, the feelings you experience are different. You feel compassion and concern and these feelings lead to a different type of action. You may decide to drop in on your neighbour for coffee to see how things are going.

The fact of life is that we will always interpret everything we see, hear and experience, but we need to examine our interpretation for evidence and be open to exploring other possible meanings.

5. Anger can be a defence. It can shield our most vulnerable feelings, such as disappointment, rejection and loss. It is important that we find a way to get behind our own defences and process the real hurt underneath so that we can move on.

6. 'I have only one nerve left and you're getting on it.'
Common sense dictates that we're more prone to irritation when

we're tired, stressed or hungry. Be aware of your own needs and how they might be affecting the situation. Small irritations that are ignored can build up and cause a huge explosion over something minor. Try not to let things build up.

Getting to know the impact and cost of your anger

It can be easier to recognise anger in others than to face and take responsibility for our own anger. Sometimes, we cannot face what we do not wish to see. However, if you have a sense that anger is impacting on your quality of life and your relationships with others, then it is really important that you take some time to explore and get to know your anger.

Completing the following exercise will help you to identify the various ways in which your anger is impacting on your life.

Before answering the questions, close your eyes for a moment and recall a recent time when you were angry. Stay with the memory for a moment. When you have done this, bring your attention to the past few months and try to recall any other experiences or expressions of anger you have had. It could be hot, fiery anger that you either expressed or suppressed, or it could be cold anger that you expressed indirectly or suppressed in the form of a deep-seated resentment. When you have finished recalling, take a moment to list the incidents you have remembered.

I have felt angry when _____

_____

_____

_____

_____

_____

Now consider how anger may be affecting different areas of your life by answering the following questions:

Is your anger impacting significantly on any of the following aspects of your life?

		Yes	No
1	Your relationship with your partner		
2	Your relationship with your friends		
3	Your relationship with family members		
4	Your mood		
5	How you are in your body		
6	Your self-esteem		
7	Your ability to relax		
8	Your sense of humour		
9	Your behaviour		
10	Your ability to experience or express joy		

Did anything surprise you about your answers to the questions listed?

_____

_____

_____

_____

Take a moment to write, in a bit of detail, how your anger has impacted on each of the areas to which you answered yes. If you do not have enough space here, use your journal to elaborate.

Below, we have given you some guidelines to help you get started.

1. Your relationship with your partner

When we feel angry or carry old angers from the past, our ability to be fully present and in relationship with another is compromised.

How does your anger impact on your relationship with your partner? When answering this question, it might be helpful to think in terms of impact under a number of headings, including communication, companionship, affection and sexual intimacy.

I feel my anger is impacting on my relationship with my partner in the following ways:

_____

_____

_____

_____

_____

_____

_____

2. Your relationship with your friends

Are there particular friendships that are affected by your anger? Take a moment to explore this. You could start by listing the key people who come to mind when you think about this question.

For each friend you have identified, take a moment to write about how your anger impacts on that particular friendship. Consider how it affects your ability to engage with that person and be available to them. Is your anger limiting any possibilities within the friendship?

I feel my anger is impacting on my relationships with my friends in the following ways:

_____

_____

_____

_____

_____

3. Your relationship with family members

How is your anger impacting on your relationships with members of your family? Do you avoid family gatherings as a result? Is it a silent anger or an outspoken anger? How would you describe your relationship with family members?

I feel my anger is impacting on my relationship with my family members in the following ways:

_____

_____

_____

_____

_____

_____

4. Your mood

Anger is not a stand-alone emotion, it is often accompanied by a range of other emotions including sadness, hurt, guilt, shame and fear. What impact does your anger have on your overall mood? When you express or suppress your anger, what feelings or thoughts are you left with?

When I feel angry, my mood is affected in the following ways:

_____

_____

_____

_____

_____

_____

5. How you are in your body

Our bodies express and hold our anger. Often when we are angry, we notice changes in our body. We may become aware of a change in our breathing or have a sense of getting hotter or a feeling of tightness in our stomachs. What are the signs of anger you notice in your body?

When I feel angry, I experience the following changes in my body:

_____

_____

_____

_____

_____

_____

6. Your self-esteem

It can be hard to feel good about yourself when you are holding a lot of anger and sometimes acting out of that anger. Guilt and shame can be extra burdens an angry person must carry.

How is your anger impacting on your self-esteem? What feelings about yourself are you left with when you have calmed down? Do you judge yourself and your anger?

When I feel angry, my self-esteem is affected in the following ways:

_____

_____

_____

_____

_____

_____

7. Your ability to relax

Anger and tension go hand in hand. Our muscles tighten and our bodies become tense. When we hold on to anger, it can become all-consuming, making it difficult to concentrate on anything else. We can become restless and find it difficult to sleep at night. Does your anger affect your ability to relax?

When I feel angry, my ability to relax is affected in the following ways:

_____

_____

_____

_____

_____

_____

8. Your sense of humour

When we are angry, it can be difficult to be playful or to see the funny side of things. What impact does your anger have on your ability to engage with your sense of humour? Does it leave any room for humour in your life? Does it add an edge to your humour? Do you become sarcastic?

When I feel angry, my sense of humour is affected in the following ways:

_____

_____

_____

_____

_____

_____

9. Your behaviour

Anger is a very strong emotion that can find expression in a range of different behaviours. These can include shouting, slamming doors, becoming verbally abusive, becoming physically abusive, and withdrawing from or ignoring the person or situation.

Consider the range of behaviours you engage in when you are angry. Include the different ways in which you act out your anger. Do you become loud and aggressive or do you withdraw and become silent? Some of these behaviours may have the effect of escalating the situation and some may have a defusing effect. Some behaviours may be obvious and some may be more subtle.

When I feel angry, I behave in the following ways:

_____

_____

_____

_____

_____

_____

These behaviours of mine often result in:

_____

_____

_____

_____

_____

_____

10. Your ability to experience or express joy

It is almost impossible to experience anger and joy at the same time. Anger restricts the spirit and limits our capacity to experience positive emotions. Are there ways or times when your anger blocks your joy?

My anger limits my capacity to experience or express joy in my life in the following ways:

_____

_____

_____

_____

_____

Take a moment to read over your answers. Did anything surprise you?
Make a note of any thoughts you have about this exercise.

Ask yourself the following questions: How would I like things to be?
What would I like to change about my behaviour?

_____

_____

_____

_____

_____

_____

Changing your relationship with your anger

In the following section, we will go through the steps you can take to change your relationship with your angry feelings.

Do you serve your anger hot or cold?

There are two main categories of angry responses: 'hot' anger and 'cold' anger. Hot anger is fiery and immediate. It can flare up suddenly and lash out indiscriminately. Cold anger is less impulsive – it takes its time, seething away, plotting revenge. Perhaps you move between both, depending on the circumstances. Which of these best describes how you feel anger?

Both forms of anger corrode the spirit and disconnect you from your own sense of well-being. Both use up a tremendous amount of energy that could be channelled into other, more positive, outcomes.

Below are ten steps that will help you change your relationship with your angry feelings and put you back in control.

1. **Tune in to your body**

   Your body is an important source of information about what is happening to you at an emotional level. Anger is often felt in the body even before we are aware of it in our minds. Try to become more aware of the changes in your bodily sensations that signal increases in your level of physical arousal.

   The energy of hot anger rises in the body and demands release. You may feel your heartbeat get faster or feel your neck and face become hot. The energy of cold anger moves downwards in the body. You may notice a heavy feeling in your stomach area or your upper body becoming slightly colder. When you notice these changes occurring in your body, say to yourself, 'I am becoming angry.' This process of acknowledging your anger with awareness creates the space for you to begin to take control.

2. **Extend the gap between arousal and expression**

   Hot anger is immediate and impulsive – but remember, act in haste, repent at leisure! An important step in managing your anger is to reduce this impulsiveness by lengthening the time span between feelings of anger and the expression of these feelings. Have you ever wished that you had just waited that extra few seconds? The first step in this process is to fully accept, at a thinking level, the importance of extending this gap between emotion and expression. You can train yourself to do this by slowly repeating the following to yourself when you become aware of your own mounting anger: 'I need to slow things down. I need to take some time.'

3. **Breathe out and down**

Use your breathing to slow things down and to reduce your level of physical arousal. The old advice of count to ten has some wisdom in it. Adapt it and breathe to ten! Take a deep breath, breathing in for three seconds and then breathing out for seven seconds. It's a tried and trusted way of reducing physical arousal, grounding the energy that has risen in your body and restoring a sense of balance.

4. **Think choices**

Now that you have slowed things down and created some space for yourself to think, ask yourself this question: 'What choices do I have in this situation?'

There are always choices, so why pick the one that damages you long-term? For example, you can choose to respond rather than to react. Part of that responding may be to walk away from or ignore the situation. The extent to which the other person is open or available to engage with you rationally in that moment may inform this choice. A cooling-down period could be good for both of you. Another option you have is to choose assertion over anger. Assertion is making your point in a manner that doesn't set out to offend the other person and involves using 'I' statements, rather than blaming 'you' statements.

It is the difference between the following two statements:

'I have been waiting twenty minutes for someone to take my order. I am really disappointed with the quality of service.'

'You stupid **** . You have been ignoring me for the past twenty minutes ... your service stinks.'

'I' statements can help prevent polarisation – when we go to extremes and create a gap too wide to bridge. They can also prevent a situation escalating. Ways of becoming more assertive will be explored in Chapter 14.

5. Take control

The expression 'out of control' is often used when referring to someone's outbursts of anger. An important step in controlling your expression of anger is to realise that *you* have full control of what you say and do – not your anger and not the other person. Taking control doesn't mean suppressing your anger

– biting your tongue is rarely effective and always painful – it means not responding to others' attempts to escalate the situation. For example, not being drawn into a competitive battle of insult trading.

Recently, I witnessed two drivers arguing over a parking space. It started with one calling the other an idiot. Inevitably, the other responded by saying, 'You're the **** idiot.'

The insults built up, layer upon layer, until the men stood nose to nose, screaming incoherently. Meanwhile, two very frightened children looked on. Don't get sucked up in the whirlwind of another's anger. Take your power back. Take control.

6. Take responsibility

Often when we are angry, we can feel a deep sense of injustice and victimisation, but this can blind us to the part we play in building and maintaining our anger. There are many ways in which we add more fuel to the fire of our own anger. Replaying a particular scene or conversation over and over in our heads can keep our anger alive long after the incident or conversation has passed. Don't get stuck in this loop – press the stop button on that tape. Once you get out of this angry loop, you can resolve to say or do something constructive or just let the matter drop.

Owning your own displaced anger or irritation can also be an important part of taking responsibility.

Have you ever had the experience of queuing impatiently in the bank, while the cashier seems to take forever and chats amiably with each customer? Internally, you scream, *Why can't she just hurry up? Why can't she quit the small talk and do her job?*

Could your irritation with the cashier have anything to do with the fact that because you didn't get up early enough, you are running late and under pressure? The anger and frustration you feel doesn't belong to the cashier, who is trying her best to chat pleasantly with her customers and give them time. It can be helpful to ask yourself how much of your anger is about 'now' and how much belongs to some other time or person.

The classic case of 'displaced anger' is when a boss criticises the employee, who then goes home and rows with his wife, who is then impatient with the child, who is unkind to the dog. In the best of all worlds, the dog would complete the loop by biting the boss!

Another important part of taking responsibility is to become more aware of your unrealistic expectations of others. If our expectations are unrealistic, we will continually be disappointed and frustrated.

7. See the funny side

It is very hard to laugh and be angry at the same time. Your sense of humour can help you dissipate your own anger. Try to see the funny side. However, it is important that it is not used as a tool to ridicule or humiliate. It can help if you don't take yourself too seriously.

8. Be compassionate

When we are consumed by anger, we are often unable to see the perspective of the other person – indeed, sometimes we don't even see them as a person. Uncontrolled anger makes an object of another person and blinds us to their humanity. When we stop seeing the other person as a person, our labels and language become more hurtful and demeaning. Thinking of the other person as an object gives us permission to retaliate rather than respond, wound rather than engage. Sometimes we need to remind ourselves that the target of our anger is a human being and we don't know what is going on in that person's life and what stresses they are under. Connecting with your own compassionate side will help you deal with your own anger. It's also important to apply this principle to yourself. Try not to judge yourself too harshly.

9. Acknowledge your successes

A successful business person was asked if he had any regrets. 'Yes,' he replied. 'I regret that I didn't take some time to celebrate my successes.'

Acknowledging our successes provides a launch pad for even more success. When you make a change that breaks the cycle of your anger, celebrate it and write what it feels like in your journal.

10. Use your imagination

Your imagination is an important resource that can help you deal with your anger. It can be particularly useful to help you rehearse new strategies or coping mechanisms in advance, so that you will be more prepared when you find yourself in a similar situation.

Take any recent incident where you reacted angrily and regretted it afterwards. Now read over steps one to nine above and revisit the situation in your mind, but this time apply some of the skills you have acquired. See what different possibilities open up for you within this creative exercise and note how you are feeling in your body afterwards.

We don't break bad habits, we replace them. One step at a time, we replace negative actions with positive actions and practise them until they become positive habits.

Dealing with old hurts and angers

Often we carry around old hurts wrapped in anger for a very long time.

Some people do bury the hatchet but they mark the spot!

In order to move on, it can be important to ask yourself a question:
What does my anger need in order for me to find peace within myself?

_____

_____

_____

_____

_____

_____

Sometimes, the feelings of hurt behind our anger need to be heard and given space.

Does your hurt and disappointment need to be given a voice? Take a
moment to write down what you would like to say to someone who has
hurt you deeply. You could use 'I' statements to describe how you felt,
how their words or actions affected you and what you needed from the
other person at that time. You could even ask questions of that person, if
there are things you didn't understand. Even if that person is no longer
alive, it may be important that you do this exercise for yourself.

_____

_____

_____

_____

_____

_____

_____

_____

This is not something you have to show or send to anyone else, but the process of listening deeply to your feelings may help you move beyond your anger. You also may find it helpful to discuss the experience of doing the exercise with someone you trust.

Reconnecting with your passionate self

Passion and anger come from the same place within us. What would it be like if you could reconnect with the fire of your own passion? The more you learn to control your expression of anger, the more passionate energy you'll have for life, joy and love.

Describe some of the things you feel passionate about.

_____

_____

_____

_____

_____

_____

Try to recall a time or moment when you felt fully connected to your passionate side. Describe how old you were, where you were at the time and who you were with. Try to recall the feeling.

_____

_____

_____

_____

_____

_____

Complete the following statement:

If I could reconnect with my passionate self, I could

_____

_____

_____

_____

_____

Anger is an energy. It has the potential to destroy or to liberate. Tap into that energy, use it to protect your dignity and keep your relationships healthy. In Chapter 14, we will look at ways to help you express your feeling, ideas and opinions in an assertive way that respects you and others.

Pathway Eleven

Accept Yourself

When God made Sam
He hadn't much to spare
so made him small
and hunched his back
to keep him ever like a child,
and love him more
than people who grew straight,
or so his mother said
and spoke a truth
concealed from learned men.
And God, to balance off His selfish act,
had placed within
this crooked oyster of a man
a pearl:
a singing voice
to pour out healthy notes
and shush the rosary of sparrows
on the roof.
At Christmas time,

when pillow-slip-pinafored puddings
swung from fresh-washed banisters,
elastic bands held little plastic Jesus
even in his crib;
he'd doff his cap and reverently swear
that Arthur Guinness
was his patron saint
to watch the fairy lights of indignation
rosy-red his sister's cheeks
and warm the cockles of his heart
on her furnace-blast descriptions
of the fires of Hell.[7]

Although Sam was a grown man, I had outgrown him by the time I was twelve years old. Sam had a crooked body and would never grow tall. He also had a fondness for a pint and a wicked sense of humour. I became fixated on all the things he couldn't do – would never do. He'd never play football like we did on the street. He'd never be a hero of the local club like our uncle or go to work like our dad.

When I took those thoughts to my dad, he said, 'You should hear him sing.'

Some time later, at a neighbour's wedding, I did hear Sam sing. I remember the difficulty he had climbing the steps to the stage and that the stand was too high so someone handed him the microphone. Then, he opened his mouth and my jaw dropped. He had the kind of tenor voice we heard from the gramophone. It seemed impossible that such a small body could produce such a huge, sweet and passionate sound and it hushed us in admiration.

I understand, now, that the only one who never saw Sam as flawed was Sam. He accepted himself and celebrated the gift of who he was.

Have you ever had the feeling that you, or anything you achieve, is never good enough? The sales targets you broke your back to meet weren't high enough. That essay you spent weeks working on is not quite perfect and you can't bring yourself to hand it in. Have you ever found that you can't leave the house until every square inch of the kitchen floor is washed? Or that you can't look in the mirror without finding fault?

If so, then perhaps you are suffering from the paralysis of perfection.

Perfectionism

Perfectionism is about striving and striving to reach what is ultimately unobtainable, and feeling miserable and disappointed as a result. Perfectionists set impossibly high standards for themselves and others and are extremely self-critical. Nothing is good enough unless it is 100 per cent – and even then ...

Of course, a certain amount of striving can be very motivating and empowering – Who wouldn't want to achieve the highest marks in the class? Who wouldn't want to run the race in the fastest time? – but, there is a difference between setting high standards and trying to achieve them, and being a perfectionist. What is the difference? One of the biggest differences is that perfectionists tend to measure their success in terms of the outcome only – it is a gold medal or nothing, 100 per cent or no grade.

When perfectionists consider they have failed, according to the unrealistic standards they have set themselves, they become extremely self-critical and this affects their mood and self-esteem. They can often become depressed and have feelings of failure and hopelessness. Even success is suspect because they tend to minimise their efforts or decide that the goal was all too easy and is therefore worthless. Perfectionists can become socially isolated – it's hard to have room for other things in your life when all your time is consumed with striving for perfection. Also, perfectionists tend to expect others to match their own standards and have little tolerance for the imperfections of others. They measure others by their own impossible standards and lose friends and alienate colleagues when nobody manages to 'measure up'.

What's the difference between perfectionists and highly motivated people?

People who are highly motivated to achieve their best are thorough and focused in their pursuit of excellence. They tend to enjoy the journey and they are not blind to everything and everyone along the way. They are more likely to see merit in their efforts, even if they fall short of their goal. They also view their mistakes or setbacks as opportunities for learning, not as catastrophes.

For example, in the face of perceived failure or disappointment, the perfectionist will tend to say, 'I failed. I'm a loser, I'll never be any good', whereas the non-perfectionist, high achiever will tend to say, 'I'm disappointed but I really worked hard and I tried my best on the day.'

Although they may experience disappointment, high achievers have low levels of self-criticism and negative thinking, and, as a result, their self-esteem is not undermined and their mood is not impacted upon negatively.

The myths of perfectionism

There are three major myths that paralyse perfectionists.

1. **The independent state of perfection actually exists**

   The fact is that nothing is perfect. Have you ever seen a perfect leaf, flower or fruit? Have you ever met the perfect person or had the perfect friend? Even the sweetest-smelling rose has petals with defects and blotches. Does that take from its beauty?

   Everything is relative, and perfection, like beauty, is in the eye of the beholder. Traditionally, even the most expensive Persian carpets have a flaw – a deliberate error woven by the artist into the carpet. The purpose of this deliberate imperfection is to show that only Allah can create perfection.

2. **This mythical state of perfection can be achieved if I work hard enough**

   Nobody can achieve what doesn't exist – no matter how hard they try. The constant striving to achieve perfection is a sure-fire path to stress and exhaustion. When the 'perfect' parent holds up an unattainable standard to a child, that child is set on the path to failure. The 'best boy/girl in the world' is a hard standard to live up to.

3. **Perfection will make you happy**

    In fact, perfectionists are most often trapped in a vicious cycle that makes them unhappy with themselves and others. They are so locked into the mythical and unobtainable goal that they miss all the opportunities for happiness and pleasure along the way.

The vicious cycle of perfectionism

The perfectionist is trapped in a vicious paralysing cycle, like the unfortunate Sisyphus in Greek mythology who was condemned to push a boulder up a hill only to have it roll again to the bottom – over and over again.

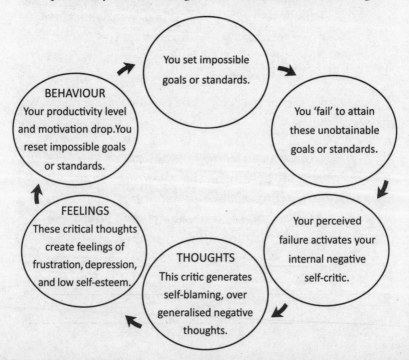

You set impossible goals or standards.

You 'fail' to attain these unobtainable goals or standards.

Your perceived failure activates your internal negative self-critic.

THOUGHTS
This critic generates self-blaming, over generalised negative thoughts.

FEELINGS
These critical thoughts create feelings of frustration, depression, and low self-esteem.

BEHAVIOUR
Your productivity level and motivation drop. You reset impossible goals or standards.

This cycle is maintained by a rigid set of hypercritical, negative thoughts and beliefs that are accompanied by feelings of despair and repeating patterns of self-defeating behaviours. Ironically, instead of facilitating and nurturing success, perfectionism actually blocks it.

To begin with, perfectionists set impossible standards or goals for themselves. When they fail to achieve their goals or standards, they interpret this failure as a sign of their own weakness or lack of ability or worth. They berate and blame themselves. These thoughts lead to feelings of despair, resentment and hopelessness, their mood drops and their self-esteem takes a serious knock. These intense feelings and critical thought processes impact on their motivation to continue, and so their productivity drops. They frequently reset the same goal or they withdraw from the task and set another unobtainable goal, repeating the cycle all over again.

Perfectionists rarely deliver the goods but they always pay a heavy price.

The cost of perfectionism

Perfectionism comes at a high price at a physical, emotional, mental and social level.

Are there any areas of your life in which you believe your quality of life would improve if you were less concerned with achieving perfection? When answering this question, consider all *aspects of your life, including work, home, study, relationships, friendships and sport.*

Describe the costs to you of constantly striving to reach impossible goals or maintain impossibly high standards in the areas you have identified.

Physical costs (stress, fatigue, health, etc.)

_____

_____

_____

_____

Emotional costs (frustrations, disappointment, depression, etc.)

_____

_____

_____

_____

Social costs (affect on relationships, friendships, recreational opportunities)

_____

_____

_____

_____

Mental costs (energy, time, worry, stress, etc.)

_____

_____

_____

_____

Now, for each of the headings listed above, consider any benefits to maintaining your perfectionism. Describe these below.

_____

_____

_____

_____

When you weigh up the benefits against the costs, is it more beneficial for you to leave things the way they are or to consider challenging your perfectionism?

_____

_____

If you think it is time to make some changes, the first place to start is to identify and challenge the thinking and behaviour patterns that are maintaining your perfectionism.

Thinking patterns that maintain perfectionism

A number of thinking errors can work together to maintain perfectionism.

Thinking error	Example
All or nothing thinking	You must achieve 100 per cent – nothing else will do, nothing else is good enough.
Labelling	When you don't achieve the goal or standard you have set, you label yourself an 'idiot' or 'useless'.
'Should' statements	You set unreal expectations for yourself and are burdened by what you perceive to be the expectations of others.
'Catastrophising'	You magnify the consequences of one small mistake or setback. 'I made one mistake, I must start over again.'
Mind-reading	You assume that other people are judging you negatively for the failure you perceive.
Negative mental filtering	You only focus on the negative and minimise or filter out the positive.
Overgeneralising	You receive one piece of criticism and you conclude that you and your work are worthless.
Emotional reasoning	You feel like a failure or a loser, therefore you conclude that you are one. You treat your feelings as facts.

In the table opposite, review the thinking errors listed above and see if you can find any examples of these patterns from your own life experience that are supporting your perfectionism. Consider all the different aspects of your life.

Thinking error	Example
All or nothing thinking	
Labelling	
'Should' statements	
'Catastrophising'	
Mind-reading	
Negative mental filtering	
Overgeneralising	
Emotional reasoning	

Behaviour patterns that maintain perfectionism

There are a number of behaviour patterns that help maintain perfectionism. These include:

- postponing or delaying finishing tasks
- avoidance
- repeatedly checking
- repeatedly correcting and revising
- not making decisions
- not delegating
- not setting time limits
- giving up
- being over-competitive
- narrowing your focus
- not allowing yourself any time for relaxation or recreation.

In the table below, describe any examples of these behaviours in the different areas of your life that may be maintaining your perfectionism.

Behaviours that maintain perfectionism	Examples
Postponing or delaying completing tasks	
Avoidance	
Repeatedly checking	

Repeatedly correcting and revising	
Not making decisions	
Not delegating	
Not setting time limits	
Giving up	
Being over-competitive	
Narrowing your focus	
Not allowing yourself any time for relaxation or recreation	

Freeing yourself from the paralysis of perfectionism

Name and shame the critic

Firstly, accept that your perfectionist striving is actually a first cousin of your inner critical voice. It sets you up to achieve the unobtainable and criticises you for not succeeding at the impossible. It is there waiting in the wings to sneer at you.

Learn the language

There is a particular type of language and set of negative statements that make your inner critic instantly recognisable. Thoughts that contain the phrases 'I should', 'I'm a failure', 'I'm no good', 'I'm a loser', 'I'm not good enough' or 'I'm useless' should set alarm bells ringing for you. These are among some of the most common thinking errors of 'all or nothing thinking', 'should statements', 'over-generalisations' and 'magnifications' that are part of the perfectionist thinking trap that is keeping you stuck.

Drop the 'not' from 'not good enough'

Talk back to your negative, perfectionist inner critic. The best way to counter irrational critical statements is to respond to them with *rational* positive statements. For example, 'It is not true that I am useless or a loser because I got a B for my essay instead of an A. I did the best I could and a B is a good mark' or 'I am too tired to wash all the dishes before I go to bed. It doesn't mean I am a failure as a mother. I can do them in the morning while I listen to my favourite music.'

Accept that there is no such thing as 'perfect', and instead resolve to try to do things as well as you can. You may not always be inspired but you can always be competent.

Fight back

Your perfectionist inner critic has a very loud voice and is quite vocal, and you need to develop some powerful put-downs to counteract that critical sneer. When your inner voice says, *You didn't iron all the laundry*, it can be very satisfying to say, 'So what?' or 'It's no big deal' or 'Who cares?' Practise saying these aloud.

Write out these phrases and place them on your fridge or save them on your phone to remind you to practise them.

Learn to separate your worth from your work

Perfectionists tend to believe that their only route to happiness or fulfilment is through achieving perfection or being the best. Their self-esteem and feelings of self-worth don't come from within but are based on the approval of others or on external standards.

Remember, your worth as a person is not defined by what you do or by what others think – or, more accurately, by what you assume others think!

Practise saying to yourself, 'My work is good enough. Sometimes it is very good, but it doesn't define who I am as a person.' Repeat this sentence out loud. Make a note of what it feels like to hear this.

_____

_____

_____

Check out your assumptions

Ask yourself if your friends or partner will think less of you because your house isn't perfectly neat and tidy or because you didn't get first place in a test or because you were overlooked for promotion. If you really can't answer this question, then perhaps you need to take a risk and ask others.

Perfectionists often tend to make assumptions about what other people are thinking – and they assume that other people think less of them when they make mistakes or fail to reach an unobtainable goal.

But because perfectionists never check their assumptions, they relate to these assumptions as if they were fact.

Try to identify some of the assumptions you make about other people that are maintaining your particular pattern of perfectionism. Consider checking out these assumptions with the person you think holds them. If you feel you can't do this directly, check them with someone you are close to and whose opinion you trust.

Search for and celebrate the positive

Perfectionists tend to zone in on every negative detail or criticism and ignore anything positive. It is a bit like being handed a ring doughnut and only focusing on the hole in the middle. When you find yourself being critical, take a moment and go in search of the positive no matter how small or apparently insignificant it is. As you do this, be mindful of the fact that perfectionists have a tendency to minimise and be dismissive of the positive.

You may have to search a little harder initially, until it becomes a more established habit. The telltale signs of minimisation are phrases like, 'Ah, but ...' and 'It was only'. For example, 'I was happy with the work I did at the weekend. Ah, but it is only a very small part of what I have to do' or 'I did get an honours mark but it was only a B.' These phrases suck the lifeblood out of positive experiences.

Practising making mistakes and adjusting your standards

It is really important when you are in training to fight perfectionism to get your retaliation in first! A great way to do this is to practise deliberately making mistakes or lowering your standards and allowing that to become a more familiar and less frightening experience. This process can help you to reduce your fear of failure and test some of the assumptions you hold about the negative impact such failure would have on your life.

Jenny was a lady with whom I worked, who set herself impossibly high standards around how she kept her home. It had to be always neat and tidy, everything in its place and impeccably clean. The pressure of this standard became a tyranny and, as a result, she lost all sense of perspective. There was no time to have coffee with friends in the morning because the floors always had to be washed and the laundry always had to be ironed and neatly folded in the hot press. In fact, I suspected she could give guided tours of her hot press. No cup or saucer was ever left unwashed and yet, with all her achievements, she experienced no sense of joy or satisfaction. In fact, she went around in a permanent state of exhaustion.

It struck me that I needed to help her create some space for herself to loosen the grip of this perfectionism.

As it happened, I was seeing her in the week between Christmas and New Year. I knew that she had been meticulous about decorating her home and, without fail, she would take the decorations down on the 5th of January. I suggested that she didn't take down the decorations on the 5th, and that she should leave them up a bit longer. We would review this each week and see if we needed to extend the deadline.

At first she couldn't bear it. She would go to the tree several times a day, touch the decorations and imagine putting them away. She told me that she had to repeatedly drag herself away by reminding herself of the promise she had made. She didn't invite anyone into her home because she was ashamed of the fact that the decorations were still up – she felt people would think she was lazy and useless.

Then, one day, a friend called in unexpectedly and they chatted for ages over coffee. Jenny's friend didn't even think about the tree and the decorations as they swapped stories and caught up on news. As her friend was leaving, Jenny pointed to the tree and the decorations in the hall and told her about the experiment she was carrying out. They both laughed heartily as her friend said, 'If you still have a burning desire to take down decorations, come over to my house at the weekend because I haven't taken mine down yet!'

Over the weeks that followed, Jenny began to spend less energy and time on housework and more time doing things she really enjoyed. Her eyes began to look brighter and the spring came back into her step. In the end, it was well into March when we both decided the experiment had served its purpose and the decorations could be put away. She smiled as she told me she would leave one bauble in the corner of the living room, both as a reminder and a cause of celebration.

Are there any deliberate mistakes or lowering of your perfectionist standards you could allow yourself to make? Take a moment to brainstorm some ideas below. Just write whatever comes into your mind, no matter how difficult or impossible it may seem.

_____

_____

_____

_____

Pick one thing from your list and try to describe what it might feel like if you could allow yourself to do this one thing.

_____

_____

_____

_____

What do you imagine would be the worst that could happen?

_____

_____

_____

_____

What do you imagine would be the benefits for you if you could loosen this perfectionist standard or behaviour?

_____

_____

_____

_____

Devise a plan to carry out this deliberate mistake or to lower your perfectionist standards. Describe what you will do and when.

_____

_____

_____

_____

When you have completed the task, make a note of what happens in your thoughts and your feelings and compare them to what you predicted might happen.

_____

_____

_____

_____

Embrace your imperfections

We don't always get everything right; it is part of who we are.

Sometimes, our imperfections and mistakes are there to remind us of our humanity and to caution us about taking ourselves too seriously.

A number of years ago I walked into the kitchen at work for a cup of coffee after a very busy morning. It was a cold day and I was wearing a warm jumper. My colleague's eyes widened as she pointed out that not only was my jumper inside out but it was back to front. I often smile as I think of the clients that I had seen that morning and wonder if they noticed. It reminds me not to take myself too seriously.

Treat your actual mistakes with respect

For perfectionists, mistakes are the enemy, a constant source of shame and disappointment. In order to free yourself from the paralysis of this way of thinking, practise relating to your mistakes differently.

Mistakes are opportunities for experiential learning and reflection. In the song 'Anthem' Leonard Cohen encourages us to celebrate the cracks that are in everything; after all, that's how the light gets in. Let some light in on your perfectionism.

Ask yourself what you can learn from mistakes – not only in terms of the task itself, but also about yourself. If you were to do the same task again, what would you do differently?

Think back on a recent mistake you feel you made that really upset you. In the space below, describe it briefly. Make a note of how you felt at the time, how you behaved and what you were thinking. When you have done this, make a list of all the things that you can learn from this mistake about yourself and the task. Ask yourself if there is anything you might do differently with this new learning.

_____

_____

_____

_____

_____

Make a note of any feelings or thoughts you have when you have completed this exercise.

_____

_____

_____

_____

_____

Set goals that are realistic and obtainable

Changing your behaviour and setting realistic goals and standards is not about having no standards or expectations of yourself – it is about loosening the tyrannical grip of perfectionism that can stop you achieving at any meaningful level.

Pick one area of your life that you would like to make a change in. Firstly identify what your normal perfectionist standard is and then set a more realistic goal. For example, at work your perfectionist standard might be that everything always has to be done your way (which is, of course, perfectly). The behaviours that maintain this are the fact that you never delegate to anyone else and you constantly check and recheck everything, which means you actually get very little done. Setting a realistic goal around this example would involve both increasing how many tasks you delegate and reducing your checking activity.

Describe below the particular goal or standard you want to adjust.

_____

_____

_____

_____

_____

*Check that these goals don't contain any 'should's or 'must's. If they do,
replace all the 'should's or 'must's with:* 'It would be nice if I ...'

_____

_____

_____

_____

*When you have done this, look at other areas of your life and don't
forget to include goals for your social and personal life, as well as for
your work or study life. If you are not sure if your goals are realistic
and obtainable, check them out with a close friend whose opinion you
value. Read the section on goal-setting (see Chapter 13) and identify
the supports you need to help you attain your goals.*

*Pick one goal to start work on. Break it down into the different steps you
will need to take to achieve it. When you have set your new, adjusted*

goal, identify the new behaviours you want to put in place to support this change.

_____

_____

_____

_____

Finally, allow for the fact that you may make mistakes or have to readjust your goals to allow for a change in circumstances.

Set realistic timeframes

Take two of the goals you have set for yourself and work out a timeframe within which you hope to achieve them.

1.   Goal 1._____

I plan to achieve this goal within the next

_____Hours _____Days _____Weeks _____Months_____ Years

2.   Goal 2._____

I plan to achieve this goal within the next

_____Hours _____Days _____Weeks _____Months_____ Years

Perfectionists tend to underestimate the time it takes to achieve their goals and so they don't give themselves enough time and, because of this, they set themselves up for failure and disappointment. Because you have been used to setting perfectionist timeframes, you need to adjust for this inbuilt bias. Whatever timeframe you have set for your goals, review them and extend them by 25 per cent in the space below.

1.   *Goal 1.* _____

I plan to achieve this goal within a more realistic timeframe of

(original timeframe +25%)

_____*Hours* _____*Days* _____*Weeks* _____*Months*_____ *Years*

2.   *Goal 2.* _____

I plan to achieve this goal within a more realistic timeframe of

(original timeframe +25%)

_____*Hours* _____*Days* _____*Weeks* _____*Months*_____ *Years*

When you have set the extended timeframe, don't just rely on your mind to determine if it is realistic – ask your body and your heart too.

If your body has to exhaust itself to help your mind achieve its goal, it won't be happy and the process may damage your health along the way. Trust your body to help you set a really realistic timeframe. Ask your body's opinion on the timeframes you have set.

_____

_____

_____

_____

_____

_____

And don't forget to check with your heart. Are there any emotional costs to the timeframes that you have set? Sometimes, friendships or relationships can be blocked or neglected because of perfectionism. Ask yourself if your friendships or family will suffer or have to be sidelined because of your timeframes. Take a moment to reflect on this in the space below.

_____

_____

_____

_____

_____

_____

If the answer is yes (or maybe), perhaps you need to consider adjusting your timeframe once more to make room for the relationships in your life that are nourishing and supportive.

It is also important that you set time limits for any individual piece of work that you do to achieve your goal. This will help to ensure that no single task takes over and becomes all-consuming. Allow for the fact that you need to be open to revising your timeframes from time to time, since life and the unexpected can get in the way.

Put the 'purr' back in purrfection

At this point, allow us to introduce our cat. He is a marmalade cat, with white socks and throat, and an attitude. He also labours under the name Kitty.

Kitty was named, as a refugee kitten, before we could determine his sex. Like his big-cat cousins on the Serengeti, Kitty is greased lightning when it suits him. He is quite capable of toppling a milk jug and lapping the contents dry in ten seconds. But his normal, everyday engine setting is at 'idle' – Kitty could 'idle' for Ireland. In fact, he has raised sloth to an art form. No surface constitutes an idle-free zone – a chair, lap, shelf or shoulder, all are equally comfortable idling places. Whatever the angle, surface or space, Kitty curls, adapts and settles. Then he purrs like an outboard engine.

We have it on good authority that he is a bilingual purrer; an exchange student from France, besotted with Kitty, claimed he could purr in French. Kitty has shown us how to put the purr back into *purrfection*. Perfectionists tend to focus on the end result only and miss out on opportunities for learning or savouring their experience along the way. Setting more realistic goals and timeframes will create the space for you to 'purr' more in your own life.

Celebrate small achievements along the path to your goals. The end results will be a reduction in stress and an increase in overall feelings of satisfaction and greater self-esteem.

Pathway Twelve

Learn to Live Well with Loss

My brother and I were close in age but were never in competition with one another. Growing up, it helped that I had accepted that he was athletically gifted and I was competent. On his part, he seemed to accept that study was my sport – we enjoyed each other's successes.

His going away in his early twenties wasn't part of the script I'd written for our relationship. I resented the culture that I considered had 'taken' him – and it was easier to reason that he'd been 'taken', rather than that he'd chosen to go. Every time I visited him in New York, I looked through the lens of that resentment and everything there appeared distorted because of my loss.

The following poem, 'Oh Absalom', was written out of that deep sense of loss and I'd like to dedicate it to all those who are experiencing the pain of loss because of emigration.

I saw him
Walk away from Bellevue in Manhattan
Hunched and small
Against the strangeness
And the silence
And the coldness of the people
And the echo of his footsteps on the sidewalk.
The air was thick, brown
Layered, like varnished cedar,
A coffin-lid closing down on Broadway.
Night was flooding off the river to the Bronx.
The subway trains, graffiti-stitched
Were keening tiredly for the dying day
As my brother turned a corner
And was gone.

It took a leave-taking of my own to bring me to my senses, and to appreciate my brother's eagerness to experience this new place and the richness of the community he had created around him. He wasn't granted enough years to fully savour his new life, and died suddenly one morning at the kitchen table in his early fifties, but I am heartened by the fact that we had used the time we had to grow closer, despite the distance. Now, he's just a thought away.

In this chapter, we will explore how to cope with loss by helping you to:
- recognise the many different types of losses
- understand the nature of the grief process
- be aware of the impact grief can have on our bodies, our minds and our hearts

- develop ways to help support a healthy grieving process
- know when to seek professional help.

The many faces of loss

When we think of loss, we immediately think of bereavement – the loss we experience on the death of a loved one – but we may experience many other losses throughout the course of our lives.

Over the past thirty-three years of our life together, we have, like most other people, had to face and work through many losses and disappointments. Christy's decision to leave the priesthood cast a shadow over our lives for some time. The deaths of both our fathers and close family members and, in more recent years, having to face our own mortality when we were both diagnosed and treated for cancer are just some of the losses we have experienced.

Every significant change in our lives involves some degree of loss and letting go, and grieving is how we process and integrate the impact of this loss.

Losing your job. The break-up of a relationship. Taking up the opportunity for a better job or a better lifestyle in another country. None of these things may seem like losses, but they all involve a process of grieving, a psychological letting go and integration of that loss in a way that helps us to redefine who we are and to re-engage with life from a new perspective.

There are no small losses, especially when it comes to death. Some lives are long and some are tragically short, but all loving relationships are life-long. The baby who dies in the womb can be loved and mourned as long and as deeply as any other significant relationship.

The following is an extract from a poem that celebrates the life of a baby who died before birth.

I did not die young
I lived my span of life
Within your body
and within your love.
There are many,
who have lived long lives
and not been loved as me.[8]

Acknowledging your losses

Take a moment to consider your experience of loss in your life.

   Below is a list of losses many of us have had to face at some time in our lives. Some of them may surprise you, but none of them are 'small' losses. If you don't find your particular loss on the list, add it at the end – it's as real and valid as any other.

* *death of a partner, family member or friend*
* *serious injury or illness of a partner*
* *serious illness of a family member or friend*
* *miscarriage*
* *having a new baby*
* *break-up of a friendship*
* *break-up of a relationship*
* *leaving home*
* *being diagnosed with a serious illness*
* *changing your job*
* *losing your job*
* *losing your home*
* *emigration*
* *retirement*
* *losing your independence*
* _____

Have you experienced any of these losses?

Are there other losses you have experienced? Take a moment to list the different experiences of loss you have had in your life. As you do this, consider different times and stages in your life from childhood through to the present.

_____

_____

_____

_____

_____

_____

What helped you at the time to deal with these experiences?

_____

_____

_____

_____

_____

_____

Is there anything you learned about yourself as a result of going through these experiences?

_____

_____

_____

_____

_____

_____

Are there any losses that you feel you have not fully grieved?

_____

_____

_____

_____

_____

The process of grief

When we have to deal with significant loss in our lives, we may experience, and indeed re-experience, some or all of the following feelings and reactions as part of our natural grieving process:

- anticipatory grief
- shock
- anger
- guilt
- regret
- sadness
- longing
- acceptance.

Anticipatory grief

The prognosis that had been delivered by the surgeon was bad. Her dad wouldn't see the summer, and she wept quietly as she drove home.

'Do you know what I was doing last night?' she asked. 'I was making a list of people who'd make sandwiches for the wake. Wasn't that an awful thing to be doing with my father still alive?'

In fact, it's a very natural thing to do and there's a name for it – it's called 'anticipatory grief'. Many people begin their grieving long before the person dies. During a long-term illness, it's a kind of 'growing away' from our loved one; an armouring of the heart against the pain of the eventual loss.

Waiting for someone to die is a most painful time. Emigrants come halfway around the world to 'be there' and then have to leave again for their faraway families and jobs. A daughter or son may opt to have the parent die at home with them and this can lead to many tensions and complications for their immediate and extended families.

What can we do to help those experiencing anticipatory grief? We can give them time to express their fears for the future. What it will be like for them when their loved one has gone. This is especially important for the care-giver who has sacrificed an independent lifestyle to care for a family member or partner. The dying person can easily become the total focus of this person's energy, almost their reason for living. When the person dies, they may not consider that there is any great reason for them to live on themselves. We can give any practical help that we are able and willing to give – and that they are willing to accept – so that they can spend more time with the person or, equally validly, time to take a break from spending *all* their time with them. It can be a huge contribution to give carers time out so that they can return refreshed to their task.

We also need to be sensitive to the time and space taken up by visitors. Simple things, like asking people to call in advance rather than just turn up on the doorstep, can make a huge difference to the quality time carers and family members can have with their loved one.

> *'She'll see us out.'*
> *His parting words.*
> *And yet, the feeling stayed*
> *And dogged his steps upon the stairs.*
> *Was it*
> *The way the light*
> *Filled shadow-pools around her eyes*
> *Her sometime sighs*
> *Or something in the way*
> *She spoke of summer*
> *And 'would John be home?'*

Anticipatory grief is how we ready our hearts for what is to come. However, nothing in the world can adequately prepare us for the shock when death occurs.

Shock, numbness, denial

> *I should have known*
> *death would not come*
> *with fife and drum*
> *but in the late-night ringing of the phone,*
> *the neighbour, standing awkward at the door,*
> *the neat, new-empty bed,*
> *the nurse's tone ...*
> *I should have known ...*

For many families, death is a slow process, a day-by-day dying; for others, it is tragically sudden. For all families – those who expected it, and those who did not – it is a shock.

The shock of loss can be the loneliest place in the world. A woman we know described to us how she wandered the streets of the small town in a daze having just received news of her brother's death. She stared numbly at the ordinariness of everything. How could the postman make his rounds? How could the children skip or dawdle on their way to school? How could their mothers' faces reflect only the ordinary concerns of their everyday lives? Was it possible that their worlds could revolve as usual, when hers had ground to a sudden halt?

Shock is the protective shell we form around ourselves to shield us from a painful reality and it works well, for a time. Inevitably, the truth permeates through our barriers and, when it does, a maelstrom of emotions is released, like the pent-up waters of a dam.

Knowing the truth is no antidote to shock. Most bereaved people experience shock even if they have been anticipating the death for some time. Sometimes, our minds and our bodies need to take care of themselves by shutting down. We seem to have a fuse-box built into our systems to protect us. If any news is too much for the mind, it is likely to go on 'automatic pilot'; otherwise, we might self-destruct. We become numb, withdrawn, and appear dazed and apathetic. Very gradually, the mind allows evidence of the truth to get inside our defences and, slowly, we begin to receive, process and accept the reality of what has happened.

Most often the shock of bereavement is felt in the body; we may feel cold and weak or numb. Some people are alarmed by this sense of weakness, but our bodies are geared to grieving and know how to take care of themselves. Just as our minds won't admit more reality than they can cope with, our bodies shut off an energy valve so that we don't become busily active and distract ourselves from the important business at hand.

'My only son was killed in an accident some months back,' he said. 'What will I do with the block of ice in my chest?' The man explained that he couldn't laugh, cry or feel anything except this icy pain and heaviness in his chest. In the case of a sudden death, our emotions can be flash-frozen by the shock. And so we go through all the motions of being alive, but we're not actually 'in it'. We seem to be detached observers of our own actions. But if this didn't happen, chances are that the intensity of our feelings would burn us to the ground.

What should this man do? He needs to bring his 'block of ice' into warm waters. By this, we mean he should contact some friends he could spend time with; friends who would allow him to feel his pain, who would warm and welcome him with their love and acceptance and not tire of his need to tell his story over and over again. Not that they might hear his story, but that *he* might hear and accept the reality for himself. In time, and within the 'warm waters' of their friendship, his 'block of ice' will begin to thaw and release his frozen feelings.

Anger

We grieve as deeply as we have loved.

The death of a loved one can be a shattering blow. That fragile bubble that we call 'normal life' can burst and disappear. Our security, our very sense of ourselves, is threatened and we are afraid. 'How will I cope?' we ask. 'What will become of me?'

Our fear and devastation can quickly turn to anger.

Imagine your life as a circular pond. Most of the time, the face of the water is reasonably still. It does get ruffled every now and then with this or that – but, on this day, a huge rock dropped out of the blue and splashed into the centre of your pond. Watch the ripples spread from the centre to the edge.

Often, it's those on the edge of our lives who feel the first brunt of our anger. Ambulance and fire brigade personnel, the police, doctors, nurses and chaplains are people at the very edge of our everyday lives. We have almost no contact with them from one day to the next. But, in a bereavement, any or all of them can suddenly loom large in our lives. We may see them as representing hope – any one of them might make the difference between life and death and they can play an important role in holding our hope for a while. However, when our loved one dies, our anger can be unleashed on those frontline people who have been close to the edge of our lives – 'I could see the ambulance crew smoking and laughing outside the double doors,' one person said to us. The youngest example of this came from the six-year-old niece of a very close friend who remarked one day as we drove by the hospital, 'Those awful nurses in there killed Nana.'

Because our loss is unbearable, we can become hyper-critical of those providing the service, as well as the service itself. Suddenly, the most innocent remark or action is interpreted through the filter of our anger and we turn on people who are trying to help, accusing them of being negligent or uncaring. What's happening here? How does it happen that a normally mild-mannered person can become so confrontational? Bereavement is like an earthquake; the ground is taken from under our feet. Every earthquake affects even the smallest weakness in the ground around it. Even the smallest irritations can be magnified by the immensity of the shock.

Anger can be a force for better or for worse among siblings or among couples after the death of a child. Bystanders can be shocked by the anger they see among the members of a bereaved family. Old fights or disagreements that have been buried for years may be resurrected at this traumatic time. There may be lots of trivial hurts that have hardened over time, but it is heartening to know that the opposite can also happen. As one man said at his father's funeral, 'Isn't it strange how you can rediscover your brother under your father's coffin?' It's a sad fact of life that it often takes a tragedy to jolt us from our comfort zones and it can take a loss to rediscover and renew a relationship.

The death of a partner can be felt as a desertion, a desertion of a young wife or husband who must now dismantle whatever future they had taken for granted and parent their children alone. When you're widowed, the world seems full of couples. Couples make friends with couples. Widows and widowers often speak of lost friends – those who have ceased calling in or asking them out.

Bereavement, through the death of a partner, is a winnowing time for other relationships. Some friends come through the process to a deeper level of closeness and some do not. The ones who stay away are not necessarily callous or uncaring. Many people get stuck in their own sense of inadequacy in the face of a friend's pain and don't know what to do or say.

If friends are important to you, then let them know that and let them know how much you miss them.

The last taboo – anger at the dead

In many cultures, so-called respect for the dead removed the reality of the person they really had been, and restricted the range of feelings of those who were left behind to grieve. It also meant that the best thing you could do for your reputation was to die. This kind of 'adulation of the dead' can lead people to bury the wrong person. When we don't bury the real person, that person will haunt us.

'Parent' is a title that needs to be earned through relationship – it's not simply something achieved biologically. Remember, we grieve to the depth that we have loved. If we didn't love, then we can't be expected to grieve as if we did. So some people, naturally and healthily, can feel relieved when a parent dies. Some feel liberated for the first time in years and look forward to constructing a meaningful life for themselves. They may grieve the father they might have had, but not the man who bullied, abused or neglected them when they were kids. They buried that man a long time ago.

Guilt – anger at myself

Guilt is anger directed at yourself. 'Why was I not a better son/daughter? Why didn't I do X and not do Y?' Every human being experiences this kind of guilt. However, bereavement can bring its own unique form of guilt. There is the guilt of the daughter who gives up her own 'prospects' to care for an ailing parent. It's a familiar story. She runs a hospice upstairs for her mother and a café downstairs for the 'callers'. Among the callers are her siblings, who may be relieved that she's taken on this role and not them. Usually, the callers tend to tell her how devoted, caring and loving she is. She may have mixed feelings herself. She may be painfully conscious of the cost to herself but who can she confide that truth to without sounding selfish? Also, most people don't become different in old age or at the approach of death. If Mammy was self-absorbed and demanding thirty years ago, she probably still is – or is better at it now after thirty years' practice.

After one funeral, when the callers were gone, I suggested to the minder/daughter that the minding must have been difficult sometimes. I remember she checked over my shoulder to make sure the callers were out of earshot before she replied, 'There were times when I could have smothered her.'

There is also the guilt of the person who survived. Why was it not me that was taken? These feelings of guilt are all part of our attempts to make sense of and integrate what has happened.

Whatever is closest to the death is most deeply embedded in the spirit.

People who work in war-zones tell of the devastation caused by a small object because it was so close to the explosion. In a loss, the most ordinary and insignificant thought, word or action can be blown out of all proportion by its nearness to the death.

Regret

What would you do if you had your life all over again? Most of us would say or unsay, do or undo things that we regret we have or haven't said or done. What can we do when we can't get the time back? The person has gone and that opportunity has passed.

We must learn to face and accept a very important truth. We are human. Sometimes we get things reasonably right and sometimes we get them spectacularly wrong. Facing and accepting that fact doesn't take away the hurt we feel. Regret is a valuable part of the human condition. Our regret provides a way for us to access the past, so that we can learn from our behaviour and invest that learning in the present.

Memories can be the most precious bequest of the departed. They leave us warm, happy, loving memories to promote our healing and nourish our spirits and they leave us some guilt memories to enhance our awareness of what matters so that we are more able and present to others in our lives.

Do we get over guilt or recover from it? In time, we learn to face our regrets, feel our sadness around them and find a balanced perception of them that we can live well with.

Talking it out and having someone really listen to you is very important when we are carrying that kind of anger at ourselves. To grieve well means to grieve honestly – and this means to be whatever way you are at any particular time without explanation or apology; to be true to your feelings, however awful or even frightening these feelings may be. To grieve well means to grieve the real person you have lost and the real relationship you had with them. It means to look honestly at the light and shadow of that relationship and decide what to let go of and what to carry forward into your new life.

Fifty years ago, I was faced with a choice. I could walk a further ten paces to my grandfather's door and tell him about the game we'd won, or I could slip into my own home and go to bed. I was tired, sore and fourteen. I chose bed. Fifty years on, my head understands why the boy chose that option but the man still remembers and feels guilty.

Fifty years is long enough to let me reflect and come to the conclusion that there was a lot more to Pop and me than a single missed visit.

> *I lastly took my pen*
> *to write the praises*
> *of a man I loved*
> *above all others,*
> *save my father,*
> *and never wrote a single word ...*
> *I laid the pen aside,*
> *Happy that years and miles*
> *Had not diminished that passion*
> *to a memory.*[9]

Sadness

They had never really been friends of ours; just nice neighbours. They'd knock at the door and ask, 'Do you need anything?'

'No, thank you,' I'd say, and close the door.

They'd be back again, a few days later. 'We're going to the shopping centre, will you come?'

'No, thank you.'

Looking back on it now, it was very rude, but I was beyond caring. They came back again, and again and again. I realise now that the only time that air and light got into the house was when I opened the door to them.

One evening they phoned and said, 'We're going for a pizza. Will you come?'

'Yes,' I said. I don't know which of us got the greater shock.

They came and we went to the pizza parlour. We talked about all the ordinary stuff. I remember, in the middle of it all, hearing someone laugh and being surprised that it was me. The evening was going wonderfully until the waiter came to take our order. He glanced at the empty chair beside me and asked, 'Are you waiting for someone, Madam?'

I burst into tears. The waiter vanished and my neighbour handed me a tissue. I told them how sad I was and they listened. Then I went to the Ladies and fixed my face and came back to eat the pizza. At the end of the evening, they invited me to their house for a coffee to round off the evening.

'Maybe sometime when I feel better,' I said.

'Well,' Nora said, 'if you come now, you'll feel better
and it'll be easier to come the next time.'

The next time? I thought. I might!

Sadness is the deep pain we feel in our hearts when the shock subsides
and we begin to fully receive in our hearts the awful reality of what has
happened – the realisation that we are waiting and waiting for someone
who will never return. Deep sadness can be accompanied by hopelessness,
despair and depression and it is important that we allow ourselves make
room for those feelings. We need to speak our pain, share our tears and
access the range of supports available to us to enable us to heal the pain
of sadness.

How long does sadness last?

Who can say? For some, it diminishes, over time, but never quite
disappears. It is a state the bereaved can return to many times.

> *I listen for his step*
> *the way he stamped his feet outside the door.*
> *I set two places as before.*
> *But now,*
> *all colour's gone,*
> *a world of grey*
> *my day to day ...*

Longing and holding

By the time we see the light from some of the stars in the night sky, the
stars themselves have ceased to exist. But they are so far away that we
still see the light they sent before they died.

Tragedies happen to other people, or so Julie believed before
the call from the hospital. For a long time, she refused to accept the
fact that the young husband who had whistled off to work that fateful

morning would not be coming back. 'Like all couples,' she said, 'we had our in-jokes, little comic rituals we would act out for fun. John had a diesel engine in his car and from five o'clock each day I listened for it. Before he turned into the garage, I would whip off the apron, pick up my compact and do a fast bit of panel-beating with powder and paint. Then, I'd strike a pose in the kitchen as he walked through the door ...'

A month after John's death, a near-neighbour bought a diesel-engine car. Even now, almost a year later, when Julie hears that sound she reaches automatically for her compact.

Why? Because she has phantom pains.

We know that people who lose a leg or an arm can still 'feel' the limb for some time. They may even feel pain in fingers and toes they no longer possess. These are phantom pains; just as the brain can continue to register sensations from amputated limbs, so the heart can continue to pick up signals from those who have been amputated from us by death. We can walk to another room in the house fully expecting to find them there. We can pick up the phone to tell or share good news and realise that they are no longer there to take the call.

We relate to people through our senses and we grieve for them through our senses because each of our senses is a storehouse of memories. Remember when you were a child, how every house in your neighbourhood had a distinctive smell – except, of course, your own? You pass a bakery, one day, and are wafted back twenty years to a different time and place. There are images that stay on the inner eye forever and the feel of a particular fabric can be enough to set a whole train of memories in motion.

We live and love through our senses and we will also grieve through them.

Just as we search through our senses for our deceased, we also try to 'hold' them through objects and places we associate with them.

How many people have a mother's ring or a dad's watch? These are things we tend to hang on to fiercely. Why? Because they help us to remain in contact with our loved one and to lose these items becomes like another bereavement. The matron of a maternity hospital I know always encourages bereaved parents to bring their baby's clothes home to support them in their grieving. 'They look so perfect and feel so warm and soft, they help all the senses to grieve and should be kept as long as they need them,' she says.

Sometimes we need to have something tangible to help us remain in contact with the essence of the person we love to support us as we grieve.

Acceptance

The way of grief is for us to accept gradually that we will never see that person in the flesh again. As this acceptance forms, we begin the process of taking the essence of that person deep inside ourselves. So, in fact, the person comes closer to us and what comes closer goes out of focus until eventually their spirit and ours become one.

Acceptance doesn't mean it's all over or that we close a door on that period of our lives and continue as if nothing had happened. It is simply the acceptance of the fact of our loss and a commitment to learning from that reality so that we can live new lives. We don't 'go back to normal', we create a new normal and incorporate our relationship with the deceased into that new life.

Can we revist some of those painful emotions like sadness and anger? Yes, maybe many times. Grief is cyclical and other happenings in our lives may set any of these feelings in motion. This is natural and normal and we grieve in different ways and at different levels of intensity all through our lives. There will never come a time when our loss doesn't matter. The fact that it matters so much to us now is a sign that it will play a part in shaping our lives in the future. The grief process, when it is done wholeheartedly, expands the heart, creating a chamber that we keep for that person alone – but, the expanded heart has room for many chambers.

Suicide – a double loss

A suicide can be a massive blow to the hearts of the bereaved. In fact, to a certain extent they experience a double loss. As well as the huge loss of the person who has died, the bereaved can often see suicide as a rejection of themselves. They can feel it was a final statement the other person made when the argument was still running and might have reached a more favourable conclusion. They flounder after answers. 'Was there something we could have done or said? Was there some sign we missed or something we lacked?' *Why?* is the most often-asked question, and there is no easy or immediate answer. Many people never find an answer to this question, but learn to live with that lack of knowing. Their rage can be a measure of the depth of love they had, and have, for this person.

Marie is a woman with a son-shaped hole in her heart. She remembers being too busy to return a missed call she had noticed on her mobile phone from her son. The next day, he was found hanging from a tree near the bank of a nearby river. Marie raged as she cried – raged against the boy who had left her with such crippling grief and guilt. 'Why didn't he wait?' she pleaded. 'We could have talked later. There was nothing so awful that we couldn't have sorted later.' Now there is no later for them. But, of course, there is for her, and within her talking about and sharing her pain lies the beginning of this process.

Some families adopt a painful vow of silence when they experience suicide. A silence that can be part of a denial of the reality and which is linked to shock and the difficulty of accepting what has just happened.

It can also be linked to shame and self-blame. This silence can make it very difficult for family members to grieve and receive support during their grieving in a real and meaningful way. Secrets become burdens that can prove very difficult to carry. Even when there is a reluctance to share the truth of the death with those outside the family, it is imperative that the truth is openly acknowledged within it. This frees every member of the family to grieve freely.

Marie's son took his own life in a lonely and distressing way and, often, it is the awfulness of a person's death that becomes the preoccupation of the bereaved. We need to allow ourselves to make a pilgrimage to the deeply hurtful places in our hearts, the distressing places; otherwise, a vacuum can be created that swallows healthy grieving. While avoidance in the short term can be a coping strategy, in the long term it becomes a closed door between us and the possibility of a new relationship with the person who has died. Marie is learning to make that painful pilgrimage. She is learning to go to that open wound and rest there without being frightened away. It is a portal to her son and, through it, she will pour out her rage, her pain, her sadness and, eventually, her love. And this is where she will learn to listen as her son speaks to her broken heart through the history of their love and their relationship which goes beyond the moment and method of his leaving. If she can be supported to do this, the time will come when she no longer needs to go to that place because she will have retrieved her son and he will come home to her heart and be always with her.

How to help support a healthy grieving process

Significant loss can impact deeply on our bodies, our minds and our hearts. Below is a summary of the symptoms of grief and loss. You may not experience all of them but they are some of the normal symptoms that can occur as part of a grieving process.

Cognitive symptoms	Physical symptoms	Emotional symptoms
difficulty concentrating	loss of sleep	shock
forgetfulness	loss of appetite	despair
preoccupation	feeling weak	hopelessness
difficulty making decisions	feeling cold	sadness
repeatedly mentally revisiting events and circumstances of the loss	needing to sleep a lot	tearfulness
disbelief	tightness in the throat	longing
denial	tightness in the chest	anger
	lack of energy	guilt
	feeling of heaviness	shame
	sense of numbness	sense of numbness

If you have suffered a loss and are experiencing grief, there are a number of things you can do that will help:

- allow yourself to accept that you have experienced a significant loss
- be aware that this loss can impact on you at an emotional, physical and cognitive level and that this is all part of a healthy grieving process
- give yourself permission to feel whatever feelings you have without trying to suppress them or judge them
- understand that your feelings may change to opposite feelings, and may vary in intensity from time to time
- accept that sometimes you may not be able to access your feelings – this does not mean you are feeling nothing
- try to take care of yourself and be aware of your body's need for rest
- put aside some time each day to do a breathing or meditation practice
- put off making any big decisions that are not urgent
- accept the help and support of friends and neighbours
- allow yourself to spend time alone if you need to
- write down your feelings and thoughts in your journal
- share your thoughts and feelings with people you feel close to and trust
- don't worry about repeating yourself; it is part of how you integrate what has happened to you
- seek the help of a mental-health professional if you are finding it too difficult to cope and if you don't experience any improvement over a period of time and you have thoughts, that are more than passing, of self-harm or suicide.

Sometimes we need a companion on our journey. It's an apt word because it means 'one who has bread with me'. There is no more basic relationship on the face of the earth than that between those who break bread together. It is doubly apt because good manners forbid those who eat bread from talking at the same time. We need a companion, a silent companion, and preferably one from outside our immediate family circle. Why? Because the bereaved need opportunities to grieve. They need people to ask so that they can tell their story and in the telling put words on their pain and put form on the wasteland they are living in. The companion must also know when it is time to stand back and withdraw. Too much help can hinder or delay a return to strength.

The companion listens without offering consolation, comfort or judgement. The companion is our link with the normal world we have forsaken for a time, and keeps us plugged into that normal life.

The companion is one who is willing to accompany us to the grave and stand with us as we rage or weep or do whatever we wish to express and process our grief.

Significant bereavements are hinge points in our lives, times when we are challenged to face and accept a new reality – to feel the deep pain of loss, search for meaning among the rubble, and try to rebuild our lives and move on. Healthy grieving can lead to an expanded person, who is deeper in wisdom and compassion than before, and more able to give and receive love.

Pathway Thirteen

Dare to Dream

In the fifteenth century, a dreamer toured the royal courts of Europe asking for money to finance his dream. He proposed sailing across an ocean no one had ever crossed to find a land few had ever seen. Unsurprisingly, Christopher Columbus grew accustomed to the sound of slamming doors.

The Spanish monarchs had just pushed the Moors out of Spain and back to northern Africa and they were broke – broke, but not stupid. When Columbus came to court, he based his arguments on three beliefs: the earth was smaller and Eurasia larger than was generally believed, and Japan lay very far to the east of China. On all three counts, he was dead wrong. They gave him the money!

Every day of the voyage, he kept his dream before him while his crew plotted mutiny behind his back. He developed a talent for bargaining, cajoling and pleading. 'Just one more day,' he begged every day, buying time to continue his quest. And then, one day, he actually discovered his dream. Except, it wasn't. He had sailed for Japan, found the Bahamas and thought he was somewhere else. Another man might have had the grace to be embarrassed, but not Columbus. He was a dreamer and knew that this is how dreams work.

A dream is not a fact. It's often as vague as a hope or an aspiration and can't be outlined or costed in any way that would move bankers to back it. It often doesn't matter if the original dream is not the one discovered; the important thing is not the destination but the discoveries made along the way.

The world, as we now know it, was discovered by dreamers who set goals for themselves and voyaged beyond the limits of what was known. Like Columbus, they didn't always discover the place they'd dreamed of, but they did discover.

One of the most important characteristics of resilient people is their capacity to dream dreams, to see other possibilities even at a time of great despair. The process of setting goals for yourself across the different areas of your life is a way of ensuring that the dreams you have don't just stay at the level of dreaming. Instead, your dreams become achievable, attainable realities that enable you to live a more meaningful and happier life.

Goal setting is about stepping into your own power and taking responsibility for shaping your future. When you start to think about setting a goal for yourself in any area of your life, you are taking the first step on your particular pathway to change and growth.

What is your experience of goal setting?

How often in the past have you set goals for yourself, failed to achieve these goals and felt even more miserable than before you set the goal in the first place?

In the space below, describe your experience of setting a goal but failing to achieve that goal. Reflect on what got in the way of you achieving your goal. Looking back, is there anything that you can identify that might have helped you achieve this goal?

_____

_____

_____

_____

_____

_____

_____

_____

_____

Now describe your experience of setting a goal and achieving that goal. This can be an example from any stage in your life. Reflect on what helped you to achieve your goal and what the feeling was like when you reached it.

_____

_____

_____

_____

_____

_____

_____

_____

_____

_____

Characteristics of successful goals

When setting a goal in any area of your life, it is really important that you don't score an 'own goal' by setting yourself up for failure. In order to succeed, goals have to have certain characteristics. They need to be what is often referred to as 'SMART' goals – that is to say, they should be specific, measurable, attainable, realistic and timely.

Specific
Specific goals are more achievable than general goals. Goals should be clear and contain as much detail as possible.

Measurable
It is very important that your goal is measurable so that you know when you have achieved it. It will also help you to measure your progress along the way to achieving your goal.

Attainable
Your goal must be one that you know you

can achieve and must not depend on the participation of someone else or on events outside your control.

Realistic

Your goal must be one you believe is possible for you to achieve and not one that has been set for you by someone else.

Timely

Goals need to be set within a timeframe and have a deadline. This will help you focus and commit to achieving your goal. However, the timeframe needs to be realistic.

Before you begin to consider setting goals, complete the following exercise.

Close your eyes and take a moment to reflect on where you are now in your life, in all the aspects of who you are. Now ask yourself the following question: 'What is within me that is trying to emerge?' Stay with this question for a short while and then write what has come to mind in the space below.

_____

_____

_____

_____

_____

_____

_____

_____

_____

_____

Setting clear, specific goals is one of the ways in which you can support what is trying to emerge within you.

In the next exercise, you are invited to set short-term, medium-term and long-term goals for some of the major areas in your life. It is really important that the goals you set for yourself are exciting, motivating and challenging for you but, at the same time, are realistic and not overwhelming. For example, if fitness is an area of your life that you would like to develop, and your starting point is that you are unfit and taking no exercise at all, then it would be unrealistic to think in terms of setting a goal to climb Everest within a year! It may, however, be completely attainable as part of a three- to five-year plan.

Our goals must be close enough in terms of attainability so that we do not become discouraged, and yet challenging enough to be motivating. As you reach those attainable goals and experience the sense of achievement that comes with that success, you can review your needs and, if you wish, set new, more challenging goals.

The important point is don't start by setting yourself up for failure.

Subdividing your goals

We are more likely to achieve our goals if we break them down into smaller, more manageable goals.

The table overleaf outlines eight major life areas – work, education, recreation, health, fitness, relationships, friendships and home. Take a moment to reflect on each of these aspects of your life and consider the areas within which you would like to make changes or grow and develop.

For each of the areas you have identified, begin by completing column two, noting where you are now in relation to this area. For example, you might begin by describing the current situation and whether you are happy or unhappy with this aspect of your life. The next step is to complete column five – your long-term, one-year goal for each area.

Ask yourself the following questions: 'What is my goal in relation to this area? In one year's time how do I want things to be? What do I want to be different?'

Then ask yourself: 'In order to achieve this one-year goal, where would I need to be in six months' time? Then in order to achieve this six-month goal, where would I need to be in one month's time?'

Goal planning

Area of my life that I would like to develop	Where I am now	Within the next month, my goal is to ...	Within the next six months, my goal is to ...	Within the next year, my goal is to...
Work				
Education/ Training				
Recreation/ Leisure				

Health				
Fitness				
Relationships				
Friendships				
Home				
Other				

The more of this preparatory work you do in relation to your goals, the more likely you are to achieve them.

Getting started

When you have completed the table, consider listing the areas of your life within which you have set goals in order of importance to you. They may all be important but it is probably not a good idea to try to achieve goals in a number of areas of your life at the same time. Pick the one to start with that you feel most engaged by.

The long-term goal I have decided to start with is _____

_____

It is really important that you know how to measure your progress in relation to your goals. Ask yourself, how will I know if I have reached my goal?

I would know that I had achieved my goal if _____

_____

_____

_____

Harnessing your strengths

In setting out to achieve your goals, remember that you are not starting from scratch. You have a number of core strengths that will be an important resource for you. In Chapter 1 – 'Recognise your Resilience' – you identified these core qualities. Look over the exercises you completed and identify from your list of strengths the specific ones that will support you as you work towards achieving your goals.

Take a moment to list these strengths below.

The strengths I have that will help me achieve my goals are

_____

_____

_____

_____

Visualising success

Imagine you are standing by the bank of a river and the one-month goal you have set is across the river on the opposite bank. You really want to get across to the other side but you're not sure how to do it. You could try jumping across, but the river is too wide and you are likely to fall into the water. Now imagine that beside you is a mound of rocks of all shapes and sizes that you can use as stepping stones to cross the river. You carefully select each stone and, one at a time, you put them in place, making sure each one is secure before you set the next one down. As you put each stepping stone in place, you experience a real sense of achievement. You begin to get excited as you realise that your goal is getting closer and closer. Imagine placing the final stone in place, and anticipate the feeling as you step onto the bank and attain your goal.

Visualising the achievment of your goal can be a powerful motivating factor in helping you to actually achieve it. When you feel your motivation dipping, try practising this visualisation exercise.

Reaching your one-month goal

The one-month goal that I have set for myself is _____

_____

_____

Now break this one-month goal down into weekly and daily steps.

In the table opposite, set daily and weekly targets that will help ensure that you reach your monthly goal. These weekly targets are the stepping stones that will help you reach your goal.

Week	Day 1	Day 2	Day 3	Day 4	Day 5	Day 6	Day 7
1.							
2.							
3.							
4.							

At the end of a month, repeat this exercise for the next month as you work towards your six-month goal.

Anticipating challenges and putting supports in place

When you set a goal, take some time to consider the supports that might make it more likely that you will achieve it. For example, it may help to share the goal with a friend or family member you trust and who is supportive. It is also important to anticipate obstacles that may arise as you try to achieve your goal. Each obstacle is a challenge to overcome. Some of these obstacles may be external and involve other people or circumstances outside your control, while others may be internal ways in which you sabotage yourself.

Try to list all the possible challenges you might encounter on the way to your goal, then brainstorm creative ways of responding to these challenges. Record your solutions in the table overleaf. It may be helpful to share your ideas with a friend or family member and ask them to contribute to the brainstorm.

Possible obstacles to achieving my goal	Possible ways to overcome these challenges	Supports that will help me to overcome these challenges
1		
2		
3		
4		
5		
6		

Celebrate success

It is really important to celebrate your achievements as you reach each step along the way to your goal. As an extra motivation, it may also help to build in some rewards that are consistent with your goal as an extra motivation.

When you have achieved and celebrated achieving your goal in one area, you can then address important goals in other areas. In the beginning, resist the temptation to take on a number of goals at the same time. For each goal you select, repeat the process outlined above. You will find that success in one area will encourage you in another and you may find yourself achieving your goals quicker than you think, or indeed resetting your goals as other possibilities open up for you.

Good luck!

Pathway Fourteen

Assert Yourself

On 1 December 1955, Rosa Parks decided not to give up her seat on the bus in Montgomery, Alabama. It was the apartheid era, when buses were divided into white and coloured sections. Because the white section was full, the driver asked her to give her seat, in the coloured section, to a white passenger. Rosa refused. She was arrested for civil disobedience and she, and her case, came to international prominence.

You don't have to break the law to establish your rights as a person. However, if you feel your needs are constantly being unmet, or that someone else is either controlling your life or not treating you as a person with dignity, you may want to look at the different ways in which you can stand up for yourself. It takes courage to make a stand and the prospect of change can be frightening.

Becoming more assertive is about developing a positive way to identify and express your wants and needs within a relationship in a manner that is respectful of the other person and of the relationship. It is also about being able to say no, and knowing how to negotiate and deal with resistance.

In this section, we will look at three ways to have your needs met and to resolve conflict:

- the non-assertive way
- the aggressive way
- the assertive way.

We will explore the impact that each way has on your relationship with the other person and with yourself.

> We will also look at:
> - Why 'I' is such a powerful word.
> - How to ask for a change in another person's behaviour.
> - How to say no without feeling guilty.
> - How to deal with resistance.

The non-assertive way

If you find yourself thinking, *My mother is so demanding I have no time left for myself* or *My kids treat me like a doormat* or *My partner takes me for granted* or *My employer ignores my suggestions*, then perhaps you are not expressing your needs and are behaving in a non-assertive manner within your relationships.

The non-assertive way is the route that aims to avoid conflict or confrontation at all costs, and the non-assertive person constantly considers themselves to be confronted by a more powerful force. They feel anxious because they see themselves as the inferior or lesser person in any situation, and adapt to this reality by 'ducking and weaving', trying to stay out of the crosshairs and so avoid conflict. They rarely, if ever, question the reasonableness of what's expected of them. In relationships, they carry a permanent white flag of surrender, letting others call the shots and direct their lives.

The non-assertive person can find it difficult to express an opinion directly.

When asked, 'Would you like to go to a movie?', they reply, 'I don't mind.'

'But would you like to go?'

'Well, if *you* want to.'

Consequently, it can be difficult for other people to know what non-assertive people want or need, which makes it even more difficult for these needs to be met.

Non-assertive people tend to be self-effacing. Their tone of voice can be hesitant and unsure around their own needs and, at times of conflict, they may try to avoid eye contact, wishing to blend into the background and disappear. Somewhere in their past, they may have learned that adults approve of the 'nice' child – the one who is seen and not heard. We all like to be liked, but the temptation to grant others the final say is a strong one for the 'nice' man or woman. Having opinions contrary to a partner might just be permissible, but expressing them would be 'disloyal'.

We can also pick up myths from our culture that non-assertiveness is a form of humility and is therefore a virtue, whereas assertive people are 'pushy' or 'opinionated'.

Non-assertive people become the 'keepers of the peace', the ones who avoid confrontation by declaring, 'Peace at any price.' They suppress their own needs and place the needs and wants of others above their own. However, although their needs are suppressed, they don't disappear. They are internalised and covered with layers of disappointment and resentment. A non-assertive person's confidence and self-esteem suffer, and their anger builds up. When this happens, they can resort to passive-aggressive behaviour and manipulation to express their anger and try to have their needs met indirectly.

Passive aggression

During the American War of Independence, the Continental army learned a quick and painful lesson: if they played by the Redcoats' rules and lined up in orderly rows to exchange musket fire and cannon salvos, they would be quickly annihilated. This was the kind of war the Redcoats excelled at, and they had superior numbers. To cope with this, they decided to become snipers and saboteurs, picking off the enemy officers from long range and going behind the lines to blow their supply wagons sky-high.

That kind of response works like a charm in warfare. However, it is a very destructive strategy to employ in human relations.

Non-assertive people can build up a large supply of stored anger. They may bury the hatchet, but they mark the spot! Over time, their stored anger begins to leak into their behaviour, through sly, hidden forms of sarcasm and an aggressive manner. It is to be seen in the revenge of the wife who hides her husband's favourite golf club or in the strategy of the office worker who says nothing when, already overloaded with work, he is given a report to complete at the last moment by a demanding boss. He resentfully works late to complete the report but three crucial pages get deliberately 'lost' in the photocopier! While these behaviours may provide the short-term illusion of assertion, in fact, the non-assertive person is still left with their anger and suppressed, unmet needs. Meanwhile, their self-esteem continues to suffer and their relationships with others become tainted.

Manipulation

Manipulation refers to a range of negative, indirect methods that non-assertive people can sometimes use to try to have their needs met. These include trying to make others feel guilty, projecting themselves as victims, sulking, withdrawing, crying, and various other strategies that try to make other people feel sorry for them, including feigning illness. These strategies may provide short-term gains but, ultimately, they damage relationships and do nothing to enhance the person's feeling of self-worth or self-esteem.

Non-assertiveness and the other person

Non-assertive people often feel angry at others for, as they see it, putting them down or keeping them trapped in a non-assertive role. But what is it like for the other people? Non-assertive people are like chameleons, adapting their behaviour to whatever background presents itself, and others may feel totally frustrated by these encounters and irritated at the behaviour of the non-assertive person. They may be annoyed at the fact that all the decision-making is being left to them.

Unfortunately, they may also be delighted, since this behaviour enables them to take and maintain control and they become very resistant as the non-assertive person begins to become more assertive.

Are there any areas in your life in which you feel you behave in a non-assertive way?

	Yes	No
Work		
Home		
Friendships		
Relationships		

Are there particular people with whom you tend to be non-assertive?

_____

_____

_____

_____

Describe a recent experience where you had a particular need that you suppressed.

_____

_____

_____

_____

What feelings were you left with after suppressing that need?

_____

_____

_____

_____

Describe a recent experience where you wanted to say no but didn't.

_____

_____

_____

_____

What feelings were you left with after you said yes?

_____

_____

_____

_____

There is a price to be paid for non-assertiveness. It can cost you the last shreds of your self-esteem and the chance of any meaningful personal or professional relationship.

Being non-assertive may mean you are out of the line of fire, hardly seen and rarely confronted, but the line of fire is where the action is. While others are moving towards involvement with people, relationship and love, you're running the other way. It doesn't have to be like that. *You* don't have to be like that. You have choices. Non-assertiveness is a behaviour. All behaviours are learned – and what is learned can be unlearned.

If you feel that someone else is in charge of your life and you feel frustrated and angry, then you can gradually begin to take more responsibility for expressing your needs. The following section on the 'assertive way' will help you do this. Remember, 'I want' is so much stronger than 'I wish'. What you want, you must ask for. Wishing alone is not enough.

Deciding to take that power of responsibility for your own needs and quality of life is the first step towards becoming more assertive.

The aggressive way

The aggressive way of having your needs met is the polar opposite to the non-assertive way – it is totally self-focused, insensitive and dismissive of other people's needs, rights and feelings.

The aggressive person isn't overly concerned about the impact of their behaviour and demands on the people around them; in fact they ignore it. They are the original 'bull in a china shop', bumping into all and sundry and leaving relationships in ruins. They use their voice and their body language to generate fear and to intimidate others, having discovered early in life that this kind of behaviour works – for them.

Aggressive people thrive on conflict. They use threat, frosty silences and glaring as communication tools. They take pride in 'lighting fires' under other people and 'getting things done'. They believe that if they didn't 'crack the whip', children would become unruly, partners would never 'do a hand's turn' and employees would 'swing the lead'. The sense of power and control they experience can become addictive and is not easily relinquished. In fact, they can become punitive and vengeful when they are crossed.

Aggressive people don't leave a lot of room for dialogue. They see their style of communication as honest and direct. 'I get to the point,' they boast, or 'I'm a plain, blunt speaker.' But their 'getting to the point' means ignoring any other point of view. Their point has been predetermined; for example, meetings are convened to rubber stamp decisions they have already made. Their version of 'honest and direct' is usually at the expense of others. Aggressive people don't appreciate the difference between being honest and being blunt. They have no sense of place or timing, offering their opinions immediately, usually loudly and in inappropriate environments. They don't just 'get to the point', they stab you with it and, like all 'blunt' instruments, they can inflict massive damage.

How do aggressive people feel about themselves?

Obviously, they may feel powerful and superior but they may also feel guilty, isolated and ashamed. No one is totally unaware of the feelings of others and, in their quieter moments, they may doubt the real effectiveness of their behaviour and may be aware of the resentment and anger of others.

Aggression and the other person

The human spirit, like nitro-glycerine, doesn't react well to compression. Partners, children and colleagues can plan and, eventually, effect an exit strategy – but even the ones who stick around can turn to vengeance. Essentially, aggressive people plant minefields around themselves.

They will try to defend themselves by arguing that they get things done – and they do – but the long-term costs outweigh the short-term benefits. Their successes are 'Pyrrhic victories' – where the cost of success is not justifiable.

'But, that's the way I am,' the aggressive persons often says, as if behaviour patterns were set in concrete and they had no alternative. Generally speaking, people tend to be 'set in their ways' when their ways suit them. There is always choice. Aggression doesn't suit anyone – not the perpetrator and not the victim. The former becomes isolated and the latter becomes distanced. Aggressiveness is not something that chooses us, we choose it. We choose to behave that way – and, so, we could choose to behave otherwise. We could choose to develop a way of communicating our needs based on self-respect and respect for others. This way is called assertiveness.

Are there any areas in your life in which you feel you behave in an aggressive way?

	Yes	No
Work		
Home		
Friendships		
Relationships		

Are there particular people with whom you tend to communicate in an aggressive manner?

_____

_____

_____

_____

Describe a recent experience where you behaved aggressively.

_____

_____

_____

_____

What feelings were you left with afterwards?

_____

_____

_____

_____

Describe some other choices you could have made.

_____

_____

_____

_____

Are there people in your life who communicate with you in an aggressive manner? Describe any recent experience you have had.

_____

_____

_____

_____

How did you feel at the time and afterwards?

_____

_____

_____

_____

How did you behave?

_____

_____

_____

_____

We will now look at ways to help you move from aggressive to assertive ways of having your needs met and resolving conflict. We will also suggest ways to help you deal assertively with the aggressive behaviour of others.

The assertive way

Assertiveness is about communicating what you want or need in a way that respects yourself and your rights but also respects the rights and feelings of others. It is not about controlling or manipulating others. It is the direct and open communication of your needs or opinions without punishing, threatening, putting down or appeasing other people – basically, it means standing up for your own rights without violating theirs.

Being assertive involves being true to yourself; being true to who you are and what you believe. It means recognising that you have choices and that it is okay to make these choices and to defend your right to make these choices.

What does the thought of being able to do that feel like for you right now?

When I think of becoming more assertive in my life right now, I feel

_____

_____

_____

_____

You may be more familiar with non-assertive or aggressive styles of communicating and the prospect of change may seem scary. However, just as non-assertiveness and aggression are learned ways of behaving, assertiveness is a way of behaving and communicating that any of us can learn. With practice, we can learn to develop more positive and constructive methods of communicating our needs and dealing with conflict. These methods will help strengthen your self-esteem and feelings of self-worth and will also help you to build relationships that are healthier and more positive.

Standing up for yourself, or self-assertion, consists of expressing your needs, knowing and, if necessary, stating your rights, expressing your own opinions and feelings, and saying no to requests that you are not happy or unwilling to accept.

Characteristics of assertive people

Think of someone you know whom you consider to be assertive. It can be someone you know personally or a public figure, or a character in a movie or book. How would you describe them? How do they act, communicate and behave? How do they walk and carry themselves? How to you think they feel?

_____

_____

_____

_____

People who are assertive in their lives tend to be more confident and get a positive reaction from others.

For the assertive person, 'I want' is not a demand or a request, it is simply a respectful statement of what they expect. For example, 'I want you to turn down the volume of your music.' In dealing with conflict or differences, an assertive person tries to keep the focus on the problem and not on the personalities or behavioural styles of the people involved. They work at involving other parties in the search for a solution. Because they 'don't play power games', the assertive person never feels out of their league or overly anxious when dealing with authority.

Discussion does not become a competition, and the opinions and insights of others are a challenge but not a threat. Other people's opinions will always be important and sought. 'What do you think?' involves respecting the insights and opinions of others, while not asking them to decide the issue.

Assertive people tend to be emotionally comfortable, and that comfort is reflected in their body posture. They look more relaxed in company and have good interpersonal skills. They make eye contact and rarely raise or lower their voice at times of disagreement – they keep the tone of discussion even and avoid explosions. They are self-respecting and extend that respect to other people and, as a result, their sense of self-worth and self-esteem is high.

Seven steps to becoming more assertive in your life

Step 1: Reconnect with your true self

Very often people who use non-assertive and aggressive ways to meet their needs have low self-esteem and have become disconnected from any sense of who they really are. Non-assertive people can live their lives in the shadow of others, while aggressive people can live in the shadow of their own anger and isolation. The first step towards becoming more assertive is to allow yourself to catch a glimpse of your true self. The following exercise will help you to begin to reconnect with who you deeply are as a person.

Take a moment and, in the space overleaf, describe five of your core qualities, starting with 'I am' or 'I have'. These should be qualities that you can own with confidence.

If you are finding this difficult, you may choose five from the following list:

Generous : Brave : Humorous : Warm : Open-minded :
Joyful : Fair-minded : Honest : Curious :
Giving : Caring : Loyal : Self-controlled :
Compassionate : Committed : Idealistic : Playful : Kind :
Sociable : Thoughtful : Spiritual :
Trustworthy : Loving : Assertive : Creative :
Passionate : Forgiving : Considerate : Grateful :
Modest : Competent : Persevering :
Hopeful : Resilient : Genuine : Dedicated :
Authentic : Reliable : Wise

I _____

I _____

I _____

I _____

I _____

When you have written these five aspects of who you are, take a moment to read each one aloud. Read them slowly and with meaning.

Record in the space below any feelings you have become aware of having completed this exercise.

_____

_____

_____

_____

Step 2: Remind yourself of your rights

We all have basic human rights. We tend to think of these in terms of our civil and legal rights, and these are important, but respect for, and acknowledgement of, human rights are equally important within relationships.

The second step in helping you move towards becoming more assertive in your life is to remind yourself of what these rights are.

Some of these rights include:

- the right to be listened to
- the right to be treated with dignity and respect

- the right to make mistakes
- the right to have needs
- the right to make your own decisions
- the right to make choices
- the right to be angry
- the right to feel and express your feelings
- the right to be happy
- the right to have fun
- the right to say no
- the right to change your mind
- the right to protect yourself.

In the space below, make a list of some of the rights you have (in any area of your life) that are not being respected at this time.

_____

_____

_____

_____

The rights you have identified above also apply to others. In the space below, consider if there are any areas in your life where you feel you could be more respectful of the rights and needs of others. Being open to acknowledging the rights and needs of others is an important step to take as you move away from being aggressive in your communication and behaviour style and move towards becoming more assertive in your relationships.

_____

_____

_____

_____

Step 3: Identify your needs and wants

Being clear about what you need and want from your life and your relationships will help you prepare the way to become more proactive about achieving those needs. Humans have many psychological needs – apart from basic needs for food, water, clothing and shelter.

Twenty of our main needs are outlined in the table below. Select the ones that you can relate to as being your needs and, in the columns provided, indicate the extent to which these needs are being met in your life at the moment.

Are your needs being met?

Need	Not at all	Somewhat	Mostly	Fully
Security				
Friendship				
Belonging				
Companionship				
Respect				
Love				
Affection				
Encouragement				
Intimacy				

Sexual expression				
Personal space				
Challenges				
Achievement				
Fun				
Independence				
Support				
Rest				
Trust				
Loyalty				
Relaxation				
Other				

Take a moment to check how you are feeling after completing this exercise. Were you surprised by anything? Be aware of any thoughts or observations and record your reflections in the space below.

_____

_____

_____

_____

Being clear about the needs in your life that are not being met will help you take steps to become more assertive. Chapter 13 – 'Dare to Dream' – will also help you to set goals to work towards meeting these needs.

Step 4: Connect with the power of 'I'

The most powerful word in an assertive person's vocabulary is 'I'. Maybe you were brought up to think that using 'I' meant you were some kind of egomaniac. You may have learned to adapt to your culture by turning 'I' into 'we', or you may have found it appropriate in a company culture to take refuge in numbers and substitute 'A lot of people think' for 'I think'.

In relationships, you may have developed the habit of suppressing what you feel in order to avoid conflict or keep the peace. An important part of being in charge of your own life means taking responsibility for expressing your feelings, needs and wants, and being prepared to negotiate to have these needs met while taking the needs of others into consideration. Using 'I' statements is a powerful way to do this. It is non-confrontational and, at the same time, relationship building.

Consider a recent situation where you suppressed what you really thought or felt. Describe the situation in the space below. Who was involved? What was the situation? Describe any feelings or thoughts that you were aware of but suppressed at the time.

_____

_____

_____

_____

_____

_____

Now imagine that you are back in that situation but, this time, instead of suppressing your thoughts or feelings, you express them using only statements that begin with 'I', e.g. I feel ..., I need ..., I want ...

_____

_____

_____

_____

Now read these statements aloud slowly, and make a note of any feelings that you are aware of as you read them.

_____

_____

_____

_____

'I' statements versus 'you' statements

'You' statements are the opposite to 'I' statements and they tend to be more aggressive and less assertive in communication that 'I' statements.

If you want to own your own feelings and opinions, and so facilitate more open communication in relationships, it is important that you actively use 'I' rather than 'you'. The alternative to owning your feelings is to attack the other person, and attacking sentences usually begin with 'you'.

How often have you heard someone say, 'You never listen to anything I say', or 'You're a ...'? 'You' statements almost always create defensive responses in the listener, who usually protests loudly and, within a short time, the argument escalates and becomes sidetracked. 'I' statements will help you move away from accusation and towards assertion.

When you find yourself in a situation of conflict or disagreement, ask yourself two questions:

What do I feel right now?

What do I need?

When you practise doing this, then 'You never listen to anything I say' becomes 'I have something to say and I feel you are not listening to me right now.' Using this assertive method, 'Your way of looking at that situation is ridiculous' becomes 'I have a different opinion', or 'You're wrong about that' becomes 'I disagree'.

Recall any recent 'you' statements you made at a time of disagreement or conflict and take a moment in the space below to rewrite them as 'I' statements.

_____

_____

_____

_____

Step 5: Practise saying no

When we suppress our own needs and are silenced by the demands and intimidation of others, we say no to ourselves and say yes to others.

Grannies or parents with time on their hands, friends with cars and older sisters with extensive wardrobes are among the long list of those who are frequently asked for favours. It can be challenging to say no, particularly to someone within your family circle. Your brother wants to stay the weekend, your sister wants something of yours to wear, your neighbour wants you to collect her child from school. The pressure to be 'obliging' can build to breaking point.

It's best to establish the ground rules rather than surrendering and resenting later. Saying no is an important part of becoming more assertive and taking back control of your life. You have a right to say no to any request without feeling guilty, whether the request seems reasonable or unreasonable. When someone asks you to do something, no matter how small, they are making a request – and a request is something you have the right to refuse. If it's not something you can refuse, then it is not a request; it is a demand.

If the other person can't take you answering no with good grace, it might reveal that the relationship is built on false assumptions or expectations, and needs to move to more solid ground.

'Will you come to my coffee morning? It's for a good cause, I will be very disappointed if you don't accept.' There is no need to feel guilty if you decide to say no and don't give in to the manipulation in the latter part of that request. You also have the right to 'think about it'. This isn't postponing an uncomfortable refusal. It is simply giving yourself time to decide if you really want to do this or not. Saying no is not about being uncooperative or inconsiderate, but it is about allowing yourself to have a choice.

Often it is *how* we say no that is important. Make eye contact with the person if they are present and try to be as clear and direct as possible. This leaves less room for misunderstanding or negotiating. For example, 'I would like to help you out but, unfortunately, I can't do that today' or 'No, I'm sorry, that's not going to be possible as I have made other plans.' If the other person persists, you may have to repeat your no. 'No, it is just not possible.' If you mean no, then say no, and keep saying it, not matter how much the other person tries to persuade or manipulate you, until they get the message.

'Sticking to your guns', especially where children are concerned, is good modelling for assertiveness, especially when the rule in question is one of the basic ones.

Think of a recent experience where you said yes but really wanted to say no. Describe the situation, what happened and how you felt afterwards. When you have done this, write down how you will say no to this request or a similar one in the future.

_____

_____

_____

_____

Saying no when you mean no is important for the following reasons:

- It means that you are listening to and respecting your own needs.
- It avoids the situations where you say yes 'to be obliging' and then feel taken advantage of or manipulated.
- It helps you set boundaries for other people.
- It helps you be more open and honest within your relationships.
- It prevents the build-up of your own anger and resentment.
- It means you – and not someone else – are the one who is making the decisions about what you should or shouldn't do.

Assertiveness is about having a healthy respect for yourself. It is also about keeping your relationships healthy. Refusing a request is your right and implies that the other person also has that right. Giving yourself permission to say no helps to keep relationships adult and balanced.

Step 6: Ask for change

As well as the right to say no, you also have the right to ask for a change in another person's behaviour, just as they have the right to request a change in your behaviour. Our non-assertiveness and fear of conflict can often lead us to accept or put up with bad behaviour from others. To avoid confrontation, people often suggest that it's the other person's personality or natural state that can't be changed – 'That's his way.' We can even reason that he would be immune to change and write a script to illustrate that point. 'There's no point in talking to him. He'd just say ...' The maxim of the law is that 'silence gives consent'.

It might also apply to behaviour. If you are never told the way you behave is wrong or offensive, you may assume there is no problem – 'Why is Sean so bossy all the time?'

'That's just his way.'

And so the dialogue continues without the participation of one of the major players. Inevitably, the frustration rises until someone happens on the truth. 'Perhaps he could change his way.'

Yes, he could.

Becoming more assertive is about asking him to make that change.

There is a simple technique we have developed called the **NEAT** technique which you can follow when asking someone to change a behaviour you find upsetting or problematic.

Name the behaviour you want the person to change.

Express your reasons and your feelings.

Ask for the particular change you want.

Try to take the needs of the other person into account when negotiating a solution or compromise.

For example, your nineteen-year-old son is playing very loud music late at night and you can't get to sleep. You feel angry and frustrated. Applying the **NEAT** technique, you might approach him and say:

(N) You are playing your music very loudly.

(E) I am very tired and I am feeling frustrated because I can't sleep.

(A) Can you please turn your music off or down so I can get some sleep?

(T) I know you love to listen to your music without using your headphones, and that it sounds better like that, but if you could use your headphones now, you can listen without them tomorrow when I am at work.

Step 7: Prepare for resistance

Sometimes our efforts to change and become more assertive can be met with resistance, and this resistance can take many forms, including refusing to discuss, blaming, behaving in ways that are attempts to trigger guilt, labelling, withdrawing, developing physical symptoms (such as headaches, stomach upset, etc.), and denying or becoming verbally abusive. If this happens, it is important to stay on track and not be distracted from your purpose which is to assert your need or express your opinion. It may be that you have to repeat yourself a number of times to get your point across. If the other person leaves before the discussion is concluded, they don't take your rights with them. You have the right to be heard and to be treated with respect. You also have the right to raise the subject as often as you need to until you are satisfied that your needs are being taken into consideration.

Assertiveness is about being aware of your needs and rights and about 'saying your say' in a direct yet sensitive way. It is never about 'scoring points' or 'putting down'. When you use 'I' statements, you take control of and responsibility for your own needs, opinions and feelings. Saying no is about taking ownership of your choices and setting limits for other people. Assertiveness also involves the right to ask another for a change in their behaviour.

Sometimes, those around us can feel challenged or threatened as we begin to change. When they can learn to accept and celebrate our growth, a deeper and more real relationship can begin.

Pathway Fifteen

Decide to Forgive

The first time I met my grandfather, I was three years old. He was my mother's father and had gone to work in England after the civil war. The day he was due to arrive home, my mother scrubbed the floors and put down newspapers. We were rubbed raw with a facecloth and warned to 'stay clean'. We sat on our doorstep until a man in a brown suit and hat turned into the lane.

'Run down to him,' she said.

My brother was older and faster. He jumped up to claim Pop's arms and left the bottom part for me. Frustrated, I kicked my grandfather in the shin and burst into tears. He lifted me up to face him. 'A boy with a fine kick like that has no cause for tears,' he said.

I became his shadow. He let me use the sharp knife to cut the plug of tobacco and tamp his pipe.

'Strike the match away from you,' he instructed. 'Hold the flame over the bowl and I'll draw it down.' When my mam was sick, he taught me to play darts.

'The wall has the chickenpox,' my grandmother observed.

'The wall will be there after us,' he said, but we switched to rings.

When my mam went to Heaven, I took up residence in his lap and we said the Rosary together every evening. It was always the Sorrowful Mysteries. I could never stay awake for the last decade, The Agony in the Garden.

'The apostles couldn't either,' Pop said.

I loved reading and read for hours on the mat before the fire. 'You'll burn the eyes out of your head,' Pop said, and went back to his own book. He read cowboy books. They had pictures of a cowboy and woman on the cover. If the front of her dress hung too low, he coloured the space with a biro. He loved all sports but his passion was cards. Night after night, he instructed me in the rules of One Hundred and Ten.

'Name the trumps.'

'Five, jack, joker, ace of hearts, ace of trumps.'

'And the number cards?'

'Highest in red, lowest in black.'

I was fourteen when I thought I caught him cheating.

'You reneged.'

'I did not.'

'If you're going to cheat, I'm going home.'

'What happened?' my dad asked and I told him. 'Well,' he said, 'you can go right back and apologise to Pop.'

He was still in the armchair and the cards lay as we'd left them. I tried to say 'sorry' but I was too big to risk crying.

'It's your deal,' he said.

Forgiveness had been granted, without shame, tears or threats and we became closer than ever before.

We are all human and a central part of our humanity is that we have the capacity not only to be hurt by others, but also to hurt others deeply. When we are betrayed, abandoned, let down or abused, the wounds we feel go very deep. Harbouring that hurt can cause our pain and resentment to build up and fester. This build-up affects us, not just emotionally, but also physically. Anger, shame, bitterness, resentment and sadness are all emotions that weigh heavily on the heart.

Continuously replaying a hurtful event in your mind can keep you frozen in time, unable to move on with your life. Over time, your spirit can begin to wither under the weight of the pain you carry deep within you. Very often, it remains unspoken but it is always present.

We may wear our pain in the hunching of our shoulders, the sharpness in our chest or the tightness of our lips. In the shadow of this pain, the suggestion of forgiveness can seem impossible and almost cruel. However, if we hold on to our anger and resentment, even when our anger is justified, we are keeping our wounds alive and open. Although it may seem strange, the process of forgiveness can be a deeply healing one. If we are open to forgiving, it can free us from the power of the hurt we have experienced and loosen the grip the person who hurt us still holds over our lives.

If you have been hurt by someone, or feel guilty or ashamed of having hurt someone else, the exercises in this chapter will help you to move towards forgiveness and beyond your wounding. If you can move beyond your wounding, it will enable you to breathe into your own power, help you to let go and set down the burden you have been carrying, enabling you to reignite your vitality and connection with life.

Deciding to forgive another

Forgiveness is a gift that we can choose to give to ourselves. It is about reclaiming what the hurt we have experienced is currently claiming from our lives. It involves fully acknowledging what we have experienced and also becoming open to moving into a different relationship within ourselves and with the person who hurt us.

Step 1: Understanding what forgiveness *is not*

It is important, before we begin, to understand what forgiveness is *not* about. Forgiveness is not about condoning or accepting unfair or unjust behaviour. Forgiveness is not about reconciliation. It does not necessarily involve entering back into relationship with the other person. You may not want that, and they may not be able to offer the kind of relationship you want and need. Forgiveness is not conditional upon the other person changing their behaviour or feeling remorse. While reconciliation requires a change in the behaviour of the other person, forgiveness does not.

If we withhold forgiveness until the other person changes their behaviour, we leave all the power with the person who has hurt us. Forgiveness is an internal process. It can occur without opening or reopening direct contact with the other person. Equally it is not about trusting the other person again, because that trust may be misplaced and has yet to be earned.

Step 2: Understanding what forgiveness *is*

Forgiveness is about taking power back from the person who hurt you and engaging actively in your own healing. It is an internal process. It involves being open to two things:

- The possibility of giving up the resentment and anger that we are entitled to feel and have carried with us for a long time.
- The possibility of developing feelings of understanding, compassion and empathy towards the person who has wounded us.

Step 3: Making the decision to start your forgiveness journey

This may seem like a big ask, but take a moment to answer the following question: 'What is it like for me to continue to carry around these feelings of anger, resentment and sadness because of the hurt I have experienced?' In answering this question, consider the impact on your head, your heart and your body and on your overall quality of life.

_____

_____

_____

_____

_____

_____

Now take a moment to imagine what it might be like for you if you no longer carried these feelings inside. Imagine how you might feel in your heart and in your body, how you might think and what your quality of life might be like if you were free of this burden.

_____

_____

_____

_____

_____

_____

Remember, you are making the decision to forgive for you. Deciding to forgive is something you can decide to do even when you believe the other person is not deserving of forgiveness.

Allow yourself to take a break for fifteen minutes before completing the remaining steps. You will need to allow at least forty minutes to do this at a time when you won't be disturbed.

Step 4: Acknowledge the injustice and hurt you have experienced

To begin with, it is really important that you allow yourself to acknowledge fully the hurt and pain you have experienced.

In the space opposite, or in your journal, take some time to describe what happened. It could be a very significant betrayal of trust or infidelity, it could be an injustice you experienced at work or at home, or it might be a small, sharp word or comment that cut very deeply. It may involve someone you know or it may involve a stranger. You may be carrying a number of these experiences from the same person or from different people, and from different times in your life. If so, make a list of these and pick the one you find most upsetting to begin with or you may choose to start to work with your most recent experience.

When you finish all the steps in this section, you may wish to repeat the exercise for different people who have hurt you.

Begin by describing what happened, where you were, who you were with, what was said or done, how you reacted at the time and afterwards, along with any detail you think is significant.

_____

_____

_____

_____

_____

_____

_____

_____

_____

Next, identify the feelings you experienced at the time and any feelings you have experienced since.

I felt _____

_____

_____

_____

_____

_____

_____

Step 5: Identify how the experience has affected you

Take a moment to stand back from the experience and consider the various ways it is impacting on you today.

The following questions will help you to do this: How much time do you spend thinking about what happened or thinking about the person who hurt you? Has your relationship with the other person changed since the event? Has your view of yourself or the other person changed because of what happened? Has your view of the world changed in any way? Has your behaviour changed in any way either towards the other person or towards other people?

_____

_____

_____

_____

_____

_____

_____

_____

Step 6: Identify the advantages and disadvantages of forgiving for you

Imagine what it would be like for you if you could forgive the person who hurt you and be released from any feelings of anger, resentment or thoughts of revenge that you may be holding. What would the advantages be for you in terms of your quality of life today? Consider the impact forgiving may have on your body, your heart and your mind. Also imagine any advantages with regard to the other relationships in your life.

If I decide to forgive this person, what would open up for me in my life?

_____

_____

_____

_____

_____

_____

Are there any disadvantages you can identify?

If I decide to forgive this person, the disadvantages for me would be

_____

_____

_____

_____

_____

What if you decide not to forgive the person who hurt you? What would you be left holding?

If I decide not to forgive this person, the advantages for me would be

_____

_____

_____

_____

_____

_____

It you decide not to forgive the person who hurt you, what would the disadvantages of not forgiving be for you?

If I decide not to forgive this person, the disadvantages for me would be

_____

_____

_____

_____

Step 7: Reaffirm your commitment to forgiving

Reread what you have written in Step 6. If you have made the decision, restate your commitment to forgive at this point.

I have decided that in terms of what is best for me in my life, I am going to complete the next six steps that will help me to move closer towards forgiving (name the person) _____ .

Read the last sentence aloud and become aware of any feelings you may have at this point.

_____

_____

_____

_____

_____

_____

Step 8: Connect with your own need to be forgiven

Take a moment to remember any time in your life when you really hurt someone and regret doing so. It can be from any stage in your life. Describe what happened, what you did or said. How old you were. Where you were at the time. Name who you hurt and, if you can, describe how you think the experience affected the other person.

_____

_____

_____

_____

_____

_____

_____

Now try to name some of the feelings you were left with after you hurt the other person and some of the feelings that you still carry with you.

_____

_____

_____

_____

_____

_____

Consider what was going on in your life at the time, the different pressures you were under.

_____

_____

_____

_____

_____

_____

Describe the other aspects of who you are that were not expressed in the hurtful act.

_____

_____

_____

_____

_____

_____

Imagine that you have an opportunity to speak with this person now about what happened and that they are open to hearing from you. What do you feel you would like to say?

_____

_____

_____

_____

_____

_____

Take a moment to read over what you have just written and be aware of any feelings you may have.

As I read over what I have written, I feel _____

_____

_____

_____

_____

_____

Step 9: Connect with your own experience of being forgiven

Take a moment to remember any time in your life when you are aware of having hurt someone who then forgave you. It can be from any stage in your life. Describe what happened, how you felt and what it was like for you to experience forgiveness.

_____

_____

_____

_____

_____

_____

_____

_____

Step 10: Separate the person from the act

Bring your attention back now to the person you have chosen to forgive. Try, if you can, to separate the person who hurt you from the hurt itself. It is possible to do this without condoning or accepting their behaviour.

What do you know of their circumstances at the time they hurt you? What was happening in their lives? What pressures were they under? What do you know of their life history or their own experience of being wounded?

_____

_____

_____

_____

_____

_____

Are you aware of any other aspects or sides to this person that are different to the part of them that wounded you?

_____

_____

_____

_____

_____

_____

_____

Step 11: Be open to any feelings of compassion and empathy

Read back over what you have written in Step 10. As you do this, note any emerging feelings of compassion or empathy towards the person who hurt you and the position they were at in their lives at the time. If you become aware of any of these feelings or thoughts, make a note of them in the space below.

_____

_____

_____

_____

_____

_____

Step 12: Receiving and accepting the pain of what happened

To enable you to forgive the person who has hurt you, it is important at this stage, in the light of all the steps you have taken, that you state your willingness to receive and accept the pain of what happened in order to break the cycle of hatred. By doing so, you agree to be open to letting go of the possibility of revenge.

I am willing to _____

_____

_____

_____

_____

_____

Step 13: Forgiving and letting go

The final step is to write a letter of forgiveness to the person who has hurt you. This is not a letter that you will send, but it is an important final step in completing your forgiveness journey; a step that will enable you to let go and move on from what happened.

In this letter, briefly describe what happened and how it impacted on you. When you have stated this, if possible name any feelings of compassion or understanding towards the other person that you have become more aware of as a result of this process. Then, tell them that you have forgiven them and state why you have taken the decision to do this. Conclude by telling them that the matter is now closed and you are moving on with your life.

Dear _____

_____

_____

_____

_____

_____

_____

_____

_____

_____

_____

_____

_____

_____

_____

_____

_____

*When you have written the letter, read it over once and make a note of
how you are feeling in your body and in your heart.*

_____

_____

_____

_____

_____

_____

_____

_____

_____

_____

You may wish at some stage to share your experience of this process with someone close to you whom you trust.

Well done!

It takes courage to work through a process like this and your completion of the thirteen steps is a sign of your deep commitment to your own quality of life and well-being.

Don't be surprised if you feel exhausted. Take some time now to do something nice for yourself, something that you find enjoyable or nurturing. You deserve it. It might be to go for a walk or meet with a friend for coffee, play your favourite music, go for a swim, put your feet up and watch your favourite show on television or have a warm bath. Find something that works for you and allow yourself to have this time.

Enjoy.

Pathway Sixteen

Be Thankful

'We should be thankful for small mercies.'

My grandmother said this often, and I always wondered why. To me, her life had been dogged by hardship. Early in life, she'd divined the difference between 'want' and 'need'. 'Want' was what you wished for; 'need' was everyday reality. During the War of Independence, she slept fitfully. Whether this was because my grandfather was away on manoeuvres or because she feared the military might raid the house, she never elaborated. The Treaty that ended one war ushered in another, a civil war, where brother fought against brother. My grandfather found himself on the losing side and went to England in search of work. They spent much of their married life apart, as he toiled alone in Dagenham and sent his wages home without fail. Even in peacetime, the tragedies mounted: one son lost to consumption and two more to the emigrant ship. My grandfather's return from England was marred by my own mother's death at thirty years of age. She bequeathed four children to my grandmother, who was in her fifties. Despite everything, she was always thankful. Thankful for a sunny day, thankful for her health, thankful for her surviving children, her grandchildren and for the kindnesses and friendship of good neighbours – small but powerful mercies.

Although she also died a relatively young woman, my grandmother taught me the meaning of thankfulness. Over the years I have learned to see the value of small kindnesses and to appreciate the extraordinary in the ordinary.

Some of the things that I feel thankful for:

My grandmother, who had a broad and welcoming lap for tears and terrors. My grandfather, who provided a safe space and calm asylum when things at home were hectic. My grandaunt, Ellen, who lived and modelled gentleness. My mother, Maura, who had so few years with us, and yet has been a life-long presence. My father, Dave, who was hard-working, loving and steadfast when I chose another way.

The teachers who believed I had 'a way with words' and encouraged me to write them. The priest who shared his library and love of books. The people who gifted me with their secrets. The dying who taught me the value of the 'now'. The bereaved who shared their heartbreak and heroism.

My wife, who makes me laugh and cherishes me despite knowing me.

Our sons, who have brought such joy and challenge to our lives.

The community in which I live and which makes me feel at home.

The woods, for shy deer, occasional badgers and abseiling squirrels.

The dawn that smoulders in the corner of the garden.

The incense of turf-smoke, rising up at dusk.

The solitude of writing, the absorption of reading.

The happy sounds of those I love returning home.

And, in and out of season, in good times and in hard times, love – above all else, love.

There are a number of things you can do to help you connect with feelings of thankfulness and to develop a practice of being thankful.

Make a list of the things in your life for which you are thankful.

_____

_____

_____

_____

_____

_____

We can often take so many things in our lives for granted which are a source of nourishment and joy. It is not that we don't appreciate them, but in the busyness of everyday living, or at times when we are feeling down, we skip over them, pass them by as if they did not exist.

Close your eyes and take a moment to consider the many things in your life you are thankful for, no matter how small. In the space overleaf, list the top ten that came to mind. Even if you find it difficult, stay with

the exercise until you can find ten things to be thankful for. You might
consider aspects of your health, your friendships, family, relationships,
nature, home environment or work.

I am thankful for:

1. _____

2. _____

3. _____

4. _____

5. _____

6. _____

7. _____

8. _____

9. _____

10. _____

When you have completed the list, read it aloud slowly, calling to mind
an image for each statement and pausing for a few seconds after each
sentence. Did anything surprise you in your choices? Note any feelings
you become aware of.

_____

_____

_____

Thankfulness and positive emotions

When we experience an awareness of being thankful or grateful for something, no matter how small, we open up pathways within ourselves that enable us to reconnect with feelings of contentment and joy. These thankful feelings can be powerful antidotes to more negative feelings of hopelessness and depression. Studies carried out in the area of positive psychology have found that nurturing this capacity to be thankful and actively expressing thankfulness not only improves our sense of well-being but also is good for our overall health and self-esteem.

On many occasions in our lives, usually when we are feeling well in ourselves, these feelings of thankfulness or gratitude come spontaneously to our minds. However, depression thrives on negativity. When we are feeling down, it is difficult to see the good or hope in anything. If we have been feeling down for a while, we may need to encourage thankfulness along until it becomes a re-established part of how we relate to ourselves and the world around us.

Practising thankfulness enables us to provide balance to negative emotions and put them in perspective. Not everything in our world is bleak. Thankfulness is one of the most powerful ways we have to help us nurture and develop positive emotions, and it is these positive emotions that contain the seeds of hope in our lives. Thankfulness helps us to see the roses among the thorns. If we can allow ourselves to be thankful for even the smallest of things, we can open the door once more to hope and joy in our lives.

Take a moment to identify at least three things you are thankful for today. It may be a small kindness that you experienced, or it may be the song of a bird you heard on your way to work, or perhaps it might be the fact that you have taken some time out for yourself today. Make a note of these in the space overleaf.

I am thankful for _____

_____

_____

_____

_____

When you have written down your three things, read them aloud slowly and make a note of any feelings that you may have.

_____

_____

_____

Each evening before you go to bed, set some time aside to look back over your day and identify at least three things that you feel thankful for. Make a note of these in your journal and note how you feel as you bring these to mind.

At the end of each week, read over what you have written and, if possible, say them aloud. Consider sharing them with someone you trust and feel close to.

Unexpected thanks

I recall filming men harvesting jute from a small lake in Bangladesh. They stood, chest-deep in water, cutting the long plants and stacking them on a canoe. The heat and humidity began to take their toll as I shifted the camera and tripod from one vantage point to another. Unbidden, an elderly man brought a stool from a hut and placed it beside me, urging me to rest.

In Kenya, I observed how even the smallest gift is received with both hands and placed immediately on a table. This gesture signifies that the gift is of great value and therefore too heavy to hold.

In Ireland, the rural practice of giving some produce as a token of thanks is a rich tradition. I fondly remember giving a reading in a parish community hall and travelling home with a leg of lamb in the passenger seat of the car!

Guides in India invariably brought gifts for the crew at the end of the 'shoot'.

A dawn to dusk 'shoot' in a Buddhist temple left us longing for showers and the sanctuary of our hotel. The monk who had accompanied us all day as we filmed spoke for the first time as we loaded the jeep.

'You have been busy,' he said. 'We feel we have not met you. Please, will you come and eat with us?'

I remember being deeply moved by his comment, 'We feel we have not met you.' Our task and our professional roles had overtaken us and he was right. We had not been available to really meet him and he had not met *us*.

The supper that evening was something very special. We forgot our tiredness as the monk enquired about our lives and families and shared his life experiences with us. What had been just a job became an experience of hospitality and graciousness. Once again, we were presented with small gifts as we left and now, when I notice that banded glass ornament catch the light as it streams through my study window, I am thankful for the softly spoken monk who taught me so much in the wisdom of that simple but profound observation, 'We feel we have not met you.'

Recall an occasion when you received thanks from someone which was unexpected or surprised you. Consider what it is about the experience that touched you and made it stand out for you. What did it mean to you at the time? Make a note of any feelings you had at the time and be aware of your feelings now as you recall the moment.

_____

_____

_____

_____

_____

_____

Receiving thanks

Become more aware of how you receive the thanks of others. Do you tend to minimise what you have done and bat away the other person's thanks with responses like, 'it was nothing' or 'don't mention it'?

Recall any recent occasion when you were thanked but did not allow yourself to fully receive the thanks you were offered.

Practise fully accepting and receiving the thanks that is offered to you. Phrases like 'you're very welcome' or 'it was a pleasure' may help you do this. Try to make eye contact with the person who is thanking you. Note in your journal your experience of doing this and what it feels like.

Saying thank you

Thankfulness works both ways. It is as important to say thanks as it is to receive thanks. How do you say thank you? Sometimes when we say thank you to others, we almost throw the thanks away in an off-hand fashion. Someone opens a door for you and you mutter thanks absentmindedly as you brush past.

Can you recall any occasions when you did this? If so, describe what happened?

Become more aware not only of taking opportunities in your day to express thanks to others but also of how you say your thanks. When you say thanks, try to make eye contact with the other person and be aware of your body posture.

Note the difference this makes for you. Become aware of any difference you experience between saying 'thanks' and saying 'thank you'. Note how the other person responds when you are thankful.

Missed opportunities

Is there someone in your life you wish you had thanked?

Set some time aside to write a letter to that person to express your gratitude. You may or may not decide to send the letter but what is important is that you take the time to complete the exercise.

It could be a letter to someone who is involved in your life at the moment or it could be a letter to someone involved in your life at any time in the past. The letter could be to someone who is no longer living.

In the space opposite, make a short note of the person to whom you would like to write the letter and briefly summarise what you would like to say. Later, set aside some quiet time to write. Try to write from your heart and don't worry about phrasing, grammar or spelling.

_____

_____

_____

_____

_____

When you have completed the exercise, read the letter aloud to yourself and write below any feelings you have.

_____

_____

_____

_____

_____

Pathway Seventeen

Nourish Your Relationships

There were ten men in the maternity hospital waiting room and only nine chairs. The 'chairless' one paced the floor, measuring the tension of the other nine. One by one, we were called to the delivery room. As each one left, the others called encouragement. As each one returned, he announced 'a boy' or 'a girl', and we cheered. Total strangers, but for those anxious moments, we were connected.

When our eldest son was delivered, he looked as if he had gone a few rounds with Mike Tyson, but I thought he was the most beautiful baby I had ever seen. I felt a surge of love, fear and joy and wondered if I could ever love another child as much as I loved him. Ten years later, his brother arrived and I had my answer.

There is more than one chamber in the heart and each one we love inhabits a part of the heart that is theirs alone.

Human beings are wired for connection. We come into the world connected, and when the cord is cut, we develop invisible cords of connection with our parents, siblings and extended family. As we grow, we lengthen those cords to enter the outside world and attach new ones as we make friends and form partnerships. These relationships in turn shape and form our relationship with ourselves. Our entire lives are a series of interconnections. Some are deep and lasting, some last only a season in our lives.

Who do you feel close to in your life right now?

In the diagram below, there are a number of circles and in the middle circle there is an X. Imagine that you are standing on the X at the centre of all the circles. The circles represent how close or distant people are to you in your life right now. Place an X on the inner circle to represent anyone you feel really close to – you can place any number of Xs. In the middle circle, place other Xs to represent people who are close to you

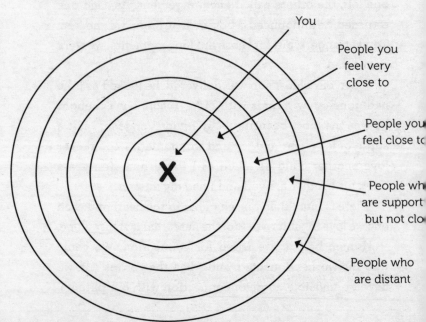

but not quite as connected, and in the next circle place an X to represent anyone who is not close to you at a personal level but who is a support to you in your life. Finally, in the outer circle place an X to represent anyone in your life from whom you feel distant or removed.

Now take a moment to identify these relationships.

People I feel very close to in my life are _____

_____

_____

_____

Other people who I feel close to are _____

_____

_____

_____

People I am not close to on a personal level but who are supportive are

_____

_____

_____

People who are in my life but I feel distant from are _____

_____

_____

_____

Now take a moment to look at the diagram and read the list you have written.

Did anything surprise you?

_____

_____

Is there anyone you would like to move from the outer circles and place closer to the inner circle? Are there any friendships in your life you would like to re-establish or people with whom you would like to have deeper or closer contact?

_____

_____

_____

_____

_____

_____

Nurturing your friendships

When we reveal ourselves to our friends, we don't do it all at once, but gradually. At the same time, they are revealing themselves to us, partly in how they deal with our revelations. Each revelation builds up an identikit picture until we are confident enough to remove our masks and allow ourselves to trust. 'Their loss', people say when someone complains of being disappointed in friendship. In some ways, it is a beautiful thing to say because it implies that offering friendship to another was the mark of a good heart and if the other failed to receive it, it was he or she who had missed out by failing to rise to a different level of relationship.

Developing friendships is not something we do lightly. In all friendships, there is vulnerability and risk as we allow people to become closer and to occupy a special place in our lives.

What are the qualities you are drawn to in a friend? It might be a sense of humour or loyalty or their interest in sport or their thoughtfulness.

_____

_____

_____

Can you identify any of these qualities in yourself?

_____

_____

_____

How would you describe yourself as a friend?

_____

_____

_____

How would your friends describe you?

_____

_____

_____

Can you identify any ways in which you could be more of a friend to yourself?

_____

_____

_____

_____

Connection and commitment

As we grow through transitions in our lives, not all our friends grow with us. Some drop away because of geographical distance or simply because they have responsibilities like our own, and order their priorities differently. Others we simply grow away from. No relationship stays static, and a relationship we found nourishing at one stage of our lives may not provide the same nourishment at a different stage. As we age, the circle of close friends tends to draw closer and is changing all the time.

Every genuine friendship involves commitment. We commit to nourishing and challenging the other in a real relationship. There are times for humouring and consoling, but our commitment is to the well-being of the person we befriend. That well-being isn't served by ignoring unacceptable behaviour, especially in terms of the friendship. Someone who takes and rarely, if ever, gives needs to be confronted with that behaviour and challenged to change. Someone who thinks friendship is possession and tries to discourage other friendships needs to have clear boundaries drawn. True friendship recognises that other friends are a natural extension and a nourishing element in any friendship.

When we are younger, we open our presents while watching what a sibling is unpacking. Comparisons are made and conclusions drawn – his was bigger, shinier, more expensive, therefore he is loved, appreciated and admired more than me. Part of maturing is realising that there is no 'more' or 'less' in love. Love is an infinite capacity that is available to everyone and can be drawn on fully without leaving a shortage for someone else. This doesn't mean that we have the same level of relationship with or the same level of commitment to everyone. Which brings us to the 2 a.m. test.

If and when you do a stock take of your friends, you might ask the following questions: Who is consistently nurturing and who is invariably needy? Who challenges and who is critical? Who turns up to help in a crisis and who comes around to witness it? Who would you call at 2 a.m. if you needed help or support?

_____

_____

_____

Do you neglect or nurture your friendships?

As a 'new' priest, I was appointed as chaplain to a hospice and four secondary schools. Zeal and the energy of youth sent me racing from one institution to another. The day never seemed to have enough hours, and exhaustion became a badge of achievement. I became oblivious to the fact that I rarely had time to keep up with a 'long-tailed' extended family. I was also blinded to the fact that I had become a flat stone, skimming across the surface of many lives and touching none of them deeply.

One day, between one crucial appointment and the next, I arrived in my sister's kitchen and declared, 'I have fifteen minutes; time for a cup of tea.' She gave me one of those looks they don't teach young ladies at Swiss finishing schools and announced, 'Here's a watch wearing a man.'

One of the major relationship-killers is busy-ness. Many of us suffer from the Bluebottle Syndrome – we buzz around frantically, headbutting the same window until we collapse. Then, we gather our scattered wits and start the same process all over again.

When did we translate 'I think, therefore I am' into 'I move, therefore I am productive'?

Constant activity can give us the illusion of achievement. A small, internal voice may warn that we are missing out on time with partners, children or extended family and friends, but too often we shut that voice down.

Take a moment to reflect on the quality of the time you have with your friends and consider if there is anything you would like to change.

_____

_____

_____

_____

Nurturing your relationship with your partner

'Only a mother could love him,' my grandmother said of someone she disliked. She didn't say he was unloved. She simply noted that it would be a challenge, a challenge that only a mother could take on. It can be a challenge relating to some people; hard to connect with them on any meaningful level. The challenge arises when we hold up the patterns we know and this particular person doesn't fit.

Whenever I told my father of my difficulty connecting with a particular person, he'd reply, 'He's someone's child.' I chewed on that for a while and concluded the person in question was hugely important to other people, even if he was a pain in the neck. As we grew older, my dad supplied a second line, 'There's a shoe for every sock.' At the time, we rolled our eyes at this folksy saying. Now that I'm older, I can accept that what I see or fail to see in another is not how someone else may see them. Those who look through the lens of love see a different person.

When my older sister started to go out to dances, we waited up to hear the 'post-mortem' on the fellows she had met and all the news of who was 'going' with whom. Sometimes, she brought her girlfriends home after the dance for night supper. As soon as we heard the hubbub in the kitchen, we slid out of the beds and perched on the landing, eavesdropping on their conversation. For a small boy, it was incredibly loud and boring. I stuck it out, waiting for a nugget that would make the suffering worthwhile, and on this particular night, they obliged.

'Did you hear about Mary?' one asked.

'No,' they chorused.

'Engaged!'

'What? Who did she get engaged to?'

To this day, I can't remember the boy's name, but I'll never forget the reaction in the kitchen. They were stunned. Eventually, one of them remarked, 'I don't know what she sees in him.'

Years later, I asked my sister if Mary had married that boy and if the marriage had worked out.

'Yes,' she said. 'He turned out to be a great husband. They're very happy.'

We may never know what Mary 'saw' in him, but I suspect she saw some quality he had managed to keep hidden from everyone else. I'm certain that she saw the best in him and gave that her love.

Whatever the light shines on will grow

Those we relate to 'see' some quality in us that is loveable and respond to it. It doesn't matter whether we feel loveable or not. Love is not earned and isn't a right. It's one of the genuine 'free gifts' we are given in life, without small print, terms or conditions.

In the modern family, the core of the family is whoever is at the heart of the home. Whether it's a couple, a single parent, grandparent, foster parent or guardian is not the real issue. The issue is that *I* or *we* are the heart of the home. If the heart is healthy, then the home will also be healthy. In terms of a couple, that means keeping their own relationship maintained and nourished.

There is no such thing as the perfect relationship or 'happy ever after'. Healthy relationships take hard work to keep them alive and vital. This is less so in the early stages of a relationship but, as time goes on, we run the risk of not only taking each other for granted but also taking the relationship for granted – and what is taken for granted withers and dies. Over time, there can also be the temptation to adopt the role of parents to the detriment of the partnership role. Time for each other is time well spent for everyone. Making time for each other is not taking time from our children; on the contrary, it reminds them that Mum and Dad have their own relationship and provides a good model for partnership.

Twenty-five positive things you can do to help nurture your relationship with your partner.

- Set aside some time every week to do things together that you both enjoy.
- At the end of each day, identify one good thing that has happened in your relationship and share this with your partner.
- Share your hopes and dreams regularly with your partner.
- Compliment your partner at least once a day.
- Celebrate both your successes.
- Fight fair – don't label or judge.
- Decide to forgive – don't 'bury the hatchet and mark the spot'.
- Be thankful and celebrate what is good within the relationship.
- Allow yourself to be playful with your partner.
- Allow yourself to flirt with your partner.
- Try not to have unrealistic expectations of your partner.
- Take time out when you need to.
- Acknowledge your disappointments and losses.
- Avoid mind-reading what your partner is thinking.
- Accept and celebrate your differences.

- Ask yourself, 'What does my partner need?'
- Be aware of and name your own needs.
- Don't assume.
- See the funny side – don't take yourself too seriously.
- Don't involve third parties in arguments.
- Share your feelings, don't suppress them.
- Deal with issues as they arise – don't let conflicts build.
- For every negative interaction, try to have at least five positive interactions.
- Tell your partner you love him/her at least once a day.
- Be affectionate. Embrace your partner at least once a day.

When people ask me when do I get the time to write books, the simplest answer is, 'You can't wait for time to arrive, you have to make it.' Having a family means becoming a time-juggler. When a juggler was asked how he managed to keep so many objects aloft at the same time, he replied, 'It helps if you heat them beforehand.' Juggling time for family, work and partnership is challenging. We met thirty-five years ago. Being together was what we always wanted, and continue to want. Two children and two careers later, a trip to the movies or a walk by the sea may not seem overly romantic, but it gives us a chance to meet each other out of role and to talk about what matters to each of us or sometimes not to talk at all.

How do you like to spend quality time with your partner?

_____

_____

_____

Would you like to spend more time with your partner?

_____

We can savour our relationship in small talk and in silence. Silence is rarely awkward for partners. Gone are the days when we talked incessantly because we needed to impress – as our relationship develops, silence becomes companionable. What a lovely word that is. Sharing the everyday bread of each other's company nourishes us as a couple. The even lovelier thing is that we remain different, unique and equal persons and our difference is what we bring to the table of our relationship.

Difference is what challenges and nourishes a relationship. Difference is one of the things we find most attractive about the other person. It's a loss to both if either person sacrifices their difference in the interests of some kind of false harmony. Harmony, after all, is a balancing of differences.

When two become one, they create a third entity called a relationship. Every first-year science student knows that if you put two parts of hydrogen gas together with one part of oxygen gas, you get a third entity called water. Push that droplet under the microscope and you'll find the two separate elements are still present in the third. Part of working at a relationship means that we work on our individuality so that we come enriched to the relationship we hold in common.

Men and women have very different styles of communication and an understanding of this difference can be helpful in a relationship. Men use conversation to convey specific information and to problem-solve. Women use conversation to make and maintain relationships.[10] Maintaining healthy relationships is about acknowledging and accepting difference.

Name some of the ways in which you are different to your partner. It could be, for example, a difference in relation to your style of communication or your personalities, your sense of humour or your likes and dislikes.

_____

_____

_____

_____

_____

_____

Name three qualities you love about your partner.

I love _____

I love _____

I love _____

Why not share your answers with your partner?

What gets in the way of relationship?

A number of things can get in the way of our relationships, including anger, perfectionism, unrealistic expectations, old hurts that are unresolved, thinking errors (that include mind-reading, emotional reasoning and labelling), financial worry and stress, poor communication and the interference of others.

Is there anything getting in the way of your relationship at the moment?

_____

_____

_____

Is there anything you need to forgive your partner for?

_____

_____

_____

Identify and share with your partner any aspects of your relationship for which you are thankful.

_____

_____

_____

_____

The old cliché holds good that nobody wants an epitaph that reads, 'I wish I had attended more meetings.' It's more likely to read, 'I wish I had spent more time with people I love. I wish I had been a better friend, lover, partner. Quality time has become a great buzz-word that can be confused with doing. Quality time can involve doing but, fundamentally, it's about *being* – being around, being available, being involved, being committed, being vulnerable, being open and being connected.

Some tongue-in-cheek survival tips for partners

- Everything we do in life is learned. If you can read, you can cook.
- A physics degree is not a qualification you need to operate the washing machine.
- Housekeeping is a partnership thing. If you think otherwise, be warned. When the serial divorcee Zsa Zsa Gabor was asked if she was a good housekeeper, she replied, 'I'm a terrific housekeeper. I always keep the house.'
- Home-cooking means whoever is at home cooks. The words 'I thought you'd never get home. I'm starving' are not conducive to a healthy relationship.

- Socks do not magic their way into drawers when they are clean or into the wash-basket after use. You do not live in Hogwarts.
- Convince yourself that vacuuming tones the upper body.
- Fight fair! 'I should have listened to my mother' is a low blow and disqualifies you.
- 'You are not the man I married' is a statement of fact, not an insult or complaint. Everybody changes.
- Nobody should be more welcome home than your partner. No matter how lousy your day has been, it always gets better when he or she walks through the door.
- Watching football or soap operas together does not decay the brain.
- Try running comments through your brain before they trip from your lips and break your jaw.
- Where you live is the only place on the planet you should call home!
- Always laugh at your partner's jokes even if you've heard them a dozen times before.
- Remember, there are only two gears in the vehicle of a partnership: forward and reverse. You are either motoring happily uphill or reversing furiously down. Either way, the partnership is moving. Handbrakes are operated only when you have arrived, and that situation should never arise.

- Preferring the newspaper reasonably intact is not a fetish.
- Never refuse a hug; you can fix the damn tap later.

If you ignore all the above, at least hold fast to this: *Speak your love often, in and out of season. Never take for granted that your partner takes it for granted. What is said from the heart nourishes both hearts and you two are a work in progress – forever.*

Pathway Eighteen

Connect with Your Community

If you can picture a kibbutz in Cork, you will have some idea of the place I come from. It was a small lane where you knew everybody's step and could determine good or bad news by its tempo. It was only when I grew away from it that I discovered the wealth and richness that were abundant there and could write of 'those who wove my Joseph's coat and left their imprimatur on that part of me I call a soul'.[11]

Our two-up, two-down house leaned companionably against the neighbouring houses along one side of a cobbled lane. The houses were so close together that we joked that if we leaned too far from our top window, we could have our tea with the neighbours! As we grew, we graduated to the lane and adventured farther to Saint Mary's Road. Beyond the tight radius of familiar lanes and streets we called The Place, there existed an exciting, alluring city we could explore with an older child or an adult as guide.

School and church were where we encountered children and adults from the other 'places' orbiting our own. Later in life, we would grow to understand 'community' in its wider definition but, for us, community began at home.

Home, to a child, is a very specific place. It's where we experience belonging and security and where we are introduced to values like tolerance, give and take, and trust; what de Tocqueville called 'habits of the heart'. The wider community ripples out from the home to include the extended family, neighbours and friends. The values we learn at home enable us to deal with this wider community and we rely on our home to model these values for us.

Like most communities, we were faced with challenges that created bonds of interdependence and mutual support. In times of hardship we 'made a little go a long way' and, often, one family's occasional surplus was rerouted to provide the basics for another.

During the war, my mother would make and pour a pot of tea for her own family and then send the pot to a neighbour who would replenish it and pour for her own. Information on where food or clothing could be sourced cheaply was freely given and received. There was a network of people within the community who would 'hang a door' or 'fix a slate' as a favour. A 'good turn' for a neighbour was something we were encouraged to do, and that favour would be returned in kind. Within the extended family, grandparents, aunts and uncles shared their lives, talents and goods, especially if one branch of the family had a particular need. I became aware of this when my mother died. After her death, we went through a period of 'miracle dinners'.

When we returned home from school our dinner bubbled happily in the pots and we served ourselves. Where did it come from? In reality, my father prepared it the night before and a neighbour checked regularly while we were at school to make sure nothing burned. The dinner appeared and the neighbour remained invisible. I can appreciate that little act of kindness now. It allowed us to feel neither different to our neighbours nor beholden to them.

Community is where we experience a sense of belonging. This is our place and these are our people. It is familiar to us, and that sense of familiarity extends from our own family to include other families until we make a network of connections; some bound close and others held lightly. We consider that network our safety net, when challenged by heartbreak, worry or aloneness. Our courage and hope come from these interlocking lines of contact and we feel assured that they will catch and support us should we fall.

Nurturing roles work both ways within this community: the old offer time and wisdom to the young, and are challenged to stay connected and young at heart by the young people, who soften their solitude.

While familiarity, with our community, doesn't breed contempt, it can engender blindness. What is closest to us loses focus. It can take the fresh eye of the outsider or visitor to refresh our own appreciation of the beauty, resources and opportunities within our community.

Rituals are the scaffolding we erect in a community to effect or support togetherness. Celebration is how we show appreciation, demonstrate affection and bring about togetherness. Celebration is even more important in hard times since renewed energy and hope proceeds from the act of celebration.

My circumstances now couldn't be more different to my inner-city childhood. Our wooded valley stretches six miles from a small town to a smaller village. Our home is one of a number of isolated houses dotted at intervals along a country road. The shop, post office and church are a drive away. Community in a rural setting can be just as closely knit, but distance can put a strain on the practice of dropping in, and it does require more effort. The danger of falling in love with nostalgia is that nothing can ever seem as good as it was. We are all tempted to look back through rose-coloured glasses at the past. But, we don't go back to the past to rediscover and recreate what was done in our childhood communities. We go back to discover 'why' it was done – what were the core values that underpinned the action? If we can discover them, then we are faced with the challenge of creating a new form for the old values.

In many cultures, every greeting and form of farewell is a type of blessing, and our culture has always valued the blessing conferred by the presence of the visitor.

An Englishman, travelling in Ireland in the seventeenth century, was moved by the hospitality of an impoverished people. Wherever he travelled, he was invited to share primitive dwellings and the little food that was available.

I recall a similar experience over twenty years ago. At the end of a long day of filming in Bangladesh, our driver invited us to visit his family. I remember squelching through mud to a ramshackle dwelling where his daughters waited with jars to pour water over our feet.

A large bed was their only piece of furniture and we were enthroned there while the family squatted on the floor. After he had introduced us, our driver presented his family, starting with his mother and then running through the hierarchy of sons, wife and daughters. Children were dispatched to neighbours and returned carrying borrowed cups for the visitors. A plate of biscuits appeared to accompany the strong tea, and I remember how thirteen pairs of eyes followed the trajectory of the biscuit from the plate to my mouth. That experience marked a shift from observation, as a film crew, to inclusion as visitors to a community. Long after we forget places we've seen, we remember the people we've encountered.

Forms of welcome change from culture to culture and from one period to another, but the value remains constant and challenging. In every household, an impending visitor leads to a big tidy-up. Whatever tensions may exist between ourselves are resolved or suspended while we address the needs of hospitality. Often, the experience of hospitality throws light on a dimension of ourselves we had lost sight of, because we can become blind to what is most familiar. In hard times, when there is less to share, the sharing is all the more valuable and enriching, as the following poem highlights.

The Stone and the Stranger

The snow had come glimmering, shimmering down.
The cold wind had wrapped it around and around
The cottage and farmhouse, the rich and the poor
As it tapped with white fingers the window and door.

And the children were hustled upstairs and to bed
While their parents discussed how the town could be
   fed.

For four winter weeks, the snow drifted and fell
Till the road from the field not a farmer could tell
Or a path from a stream or a rock from a hill
And the people grew hungry and hungrier still.
Then at last came a day when the sunlight crept
   through
And the townsfolk all came to decide what to do.
But everyone there with a loaf or a bun
Kept his heart tightly closed should his neighbour have
   none.
Then a Stranger said, 'Build me a fire in the Square,'
And for brambles and twigs they ran here and ran
   there.
'And place a large pot in the heart of the flame
And gather around,' said the man with no name.
'Neither jewels nor diamonds nor gold do I own
But my treasure is here in this magical stone.
If I wait till the water grows bubbly and hot
And I drop in this stone through the mouth of the pot
It will make this amazing and wonderful stew.'
And the people all shouted, 'Oh, do, sir, please do.'
Then lo and behold, just as quick as a flash,
They saw it soar up and drop down with a splash.
Then he dipped in a ladle and tasted the stew
And murmured aloud, 'It will do, it will do.
But a carrot would give it a wonderful taste.'
And a neighbour ran home in the greatest of haste

And he threw in the pot every carrot he had
The stranger then tasted and murmured, 'Not bad.
But an onion, an onion, one onion at least
Would give it a lift from a meal to a feast.'
And away went another to grab from the shelf
The onions he'd hung there all safe for himself.
And each time he tasted, the Stranger said, 'Good.'
Then away went another as fast as he could.
And when each had brought some and when each one
  had none
The stranger looked up from the pot and said, 'Done.'

Oh, they filled up their bowls with the magical stew
And to empty the pot gave them all they could do.
And at last they trudged homeward all happy and fed
And gave thanks for the feast and fell straight into
  bed.

When the blanket of night rolled away from the day
The stone and the stranger had gone on their way
To search in the snow for a village in need,
To make neighbours of strangers, the people agreed.

Time given to the community is a small tithe to pay for the riches we receive back. We have a lot to value in our community. We value the friends who have 'bound themselves to us with chains of steel'. We value our neighbours who grace our kitchen and our lives. We value the girl in the shop and the man in the post office and all those whose service is so much warmer than that word implies. We value the quiet heroes and heroines who voluntarily do all the things that sustain and express community values. We value those we meet and greet on the street and those who wave from passing cars, those who receive and return our greetings.

This is community.

We love spending time reclaiming our garden from the wilderness every Saturday but we are also aware of how precious Saturdays are as a time to link up with neighbours and catch up after the busyness of the week. Linda proposed we should have a garden *meitheal* – '*meitheal*' is the Irish word for a gathering of neighbours and friends to help harvest the cereal crops. The practice was popular in the days before combine harvesters, when neighbours would rotate from farm to farm and make short and joyful work of the harvest.

Every weekend, throughout the summer months, a different household hosted our garden *meitheal*. At 10 a.m. every Saturday, a motley crew of young and old, carrying various gardening implements and in various states of disrepair, would arrive at a designated garden and give of their labour and wisdom for a few hours. Tasks were allotted according to gardening aptitude, or none, and the day concluded at the kitchen table with soup, sandwiches and lots of laughter. It continued for ten years and lapsed only when people moved away, but we still cherish the friendships made and the contribution their friendship made to our family.

Over the years card games, poetry readings, book circles and carol singing have all played their part, in and out of season, in binding our local community together.

You and your community

Behind every tapestry is a rich web of colourless threads that bind the colours to the canvas. Often, it is the small courtesies, such as saluting, a greeting and a few words of conversation, that weave a community together.

Do you have any positive experiences of feeling part of a group or community? Take a moment to recall that experience. Describe the community or small group. What brought the group together and how did you become part of it?

_____

_____

_____

_____

What did it feel like to be a part of that group?

_____

_____

_____

_____

What values did the group share or have in common?

_____

_____

_____

_____

What part of you came alive within that group?

_____

_____

_____

Do you feel part of any community or group at the moment?

Are there any steps you could take to make more contact or connection with your local community, such as volunteering or joining a local club or group?

_____

_____

_____

_____

'No man is an island,' John Donne wrote. Essentially, we are individual 'islands' who join ourselves with other islands to make communities. We can opt to build bridges from one island to another, or choose to remain isolated. When we do reach out and engage with each other, all our lives are enriched.

Pathway Nineteen

Allow Your Soul to Sing

We all have a tune or a song that affects us, evoking our oldest memories and deepest emotions. In my childhood home, everyone was expected to have a 'party piece' and perform it at family celebrations. Each person had a 'special' song, and woe betide anyone who hijacked it and sang it first. My grandfather sang 'In Cellar Cool', in a deep, bass voice, while my sister Kay sang 'Black Magic', in a bluesy voice, much too knowing for her years! My dad Dave sang 'My Heart and I', and even though we were very young, we knew it was a lament for our late mother.

He never spoke to us about her death and of how much he missed her, but singing that song with its poignant line 'We are in love with you, my heart and I' allowed him to express what he could never say. He sang his song throughout the rest of his life and, without my realising it, he passed on the baton to me. It was the song I sang to Linda when we were falling in love, and one that remains very special to both of us.

Our last memory of him singing it was at our elder son's christening, at a time when his health was in decline. His voice was frail but true and there was not a dry eye in the room. We can never hear that song without reopening our connection with the man he was and our deep love for him.

Music is universal and international. It transcends borders and cultures, enabling us to make contact with the soul of a people as they celebrate, commemorate, express and evoke the deepest emotions of their own culture. In the eighteenth century, citizens of Marseille walked all the way to Paris to join the Revolution and, as they tramped along, they sang a new anthem – 'La Marseillaise', a song that can still stir strong emotions of pride and hope, even for those who have never visited France. In our own time, few are not moved by Welsh voices rising up to compete with the anthem of Les Bleus, and the plaintive rendition of the 'Star-Spangled Banner' can send a chill down the spine.

Do you have any songs or pieces of music that, when you hear them, stop you in your tracks and immediately transport you back to happier times, or connect you with someone or some special time in your life? If so, take a moment to note the song, nursery rhyme or piece of music and any memories, feelings or images it evokes.

_____

_____

_____

_____

_____

_____

Are there any songs or pieces of music from your own culture or other cultures that have the capacity to fill you with pride or make the hairs on the back of your neck stand up and salute?

_____

_____

_____

Music and mood

Music and song have an enormous capacity to reach inside and touch our emotions at a very deep level. The first music we encounter is our mother's voice, vibrating through the amniotic fluid to the backing track of her steady heartbeat. Then we are born into a world of music, a wonderful arrangement of sounds and silences. Even before we start moulding sound into words, we warble, coo and wail to express a whole range of needs and emotions.

The powerful effect of music on emotion has been noted, even as far back as the Old Testament. When King Saul slipped into one of his murderous moods, only the young man David could soothe him by playing the harp. Many psychological studies have looked at the powerful effect music can have both in terms of maintaining a particular mood or in helping us to change our mood and feel better. When we are feeling down, our inclination can be not to listen to music at all or to listen to and play music that fits our depressed state. When a romantic relationship is on the rocks or has broken down, we can be drawn to listen to songs of betrayal and abandonment that match how we feel – 'walk backwards as you're leaving so I'll think you're coming in' comes to mind! These songs can help us process and release emotions but can also keep us stuck in that emotional state if that is the only music we listen to.

Music can also help our soul to sing and soar. It has the power to connect us, even in our darkest moments, with love and life, joy and laughter. When I worked in a hospice, I saw this kind of transformational miracle at first hand. John was a man whose refuge from the reality of his terminal illness was silence. I was attempting to lead him into conversation one day, when someone turned on a radio and the most beautiful duet soared up and out to where we sat. He raised a hand to stem my flow and we sat until the last notes faded. '"The Flower Duet" from *Lakmé*,' he said quietly, 'it always gives me a lift.' On another occasion, I persuaded a harp-playing cousin to play for the residents. I remember the smiles and tears the music evoked from those men and women in the last days of their lives.

Some pieces of music have the power to lift our spirits even if we try our hardest to resist.

Make a list of your favourite songs or singers and try to identify pieces in particular that you find uplifting. Our favourites are Grieg's 'Morning' or anything by Nina Simone.

_____

_____

_____

_____

Set some time aside to listen to the pieces you have identified.

Music and love

Falling in love is one of the times when we discover just how inadequate words can be for expressing our deepest feelings. 'How do I love thee, let me count the ways' can lead to a list that limits the breadth and depth of our love. There are places within us that are beyond language, and music enables one heart to speak directly to another heart – as Shakespeare put it, 'If music be the food of love, play on.'

Many of us remember a nursery rhyme or song sung to us in childhood that captured the love a parent had for us. Most couples have a song that they call 'our song', a song that marks the time in their relationship when friendship drifted towards love. Sharing music as a couple can help to nurture and heal a relationship as both of you connect in a different way or are taken back to happier times in your relationship.

Singing to and with each other has been a very important part of our own relationship. And, yes, there is a particular song we sing – Dave's song, 'My Heart and I', and it still weaves its magic after all these years.

In the space below, identify your favourite love songs. Are there any songs or pieces of music you associate in particular with times in your life when you were in love?

_____

_____

_____

_____

_____

_____

Consider sharing this list with your partner. Perhaps they also can identify their favourite songs. Make some time and space for both of you to listen to your choices.

Music and laughter

If music is 'the food of love', then music that makes us laugh is the dessert for the soul, the something light and fluffy that tickles the funny bone and raises the spirit no matter what our circumstances. Who can resist a smile when Eartha Kitt wishes, huskily, for 'an old-fashioned millionaire'? Or when the arrival of the pompous 'Queen of Sheba' is announced. Who doesn't laugh along as Danny Kaye quacks through 'The Ugly Duckling' or gives a manic version of 'The pestle in the vessel'? And sometimes, an irreverent 'take' on a solid, old song is enough to set us off, like Jimmy Durante's discovery of 'the lost chord'. The laughter that music brings can be a wonderful distraction.

I remember being very anxious many years ago prior to having an operation on my knee. 'It's a very straightforward operation,' the surgeon assured me. Of course, he wasn't the one lying on the hospital trolley. All prepped and wearing a fetching shower-cap, I was wheeled along the corridor to the operating theatre. As the ceiling slipped by above me, I wondered why the hospital authorities hadn't hired some local Michelangelo to paint a few calming pictures up there. Nauseous, yellow paint and fly-specked lampshades did nothing for my anxiety levels.

Okay, they're going to take a tiny, crinkled, piece of cartilage from my left knee – but that was my brain talking. My heart and pulse were marching to a different drummer. We were wheeling by a ward when I heard the first lines of a song, coming from the radio. 'All of me,' Frank Sinatra crooned, 'why not take all of me?' and I started to smile. *Right song, right time*, I thought. I was still smiling when the anaesthetist loomed over me and the lights gradually went out.

What music or songs make you smile? Take a moment to write down any songs, singers or pieces of music that can make you smile no matter what is happening in your life.

_____

_____

_____

_____

_____

_____

When is the last time you listened to one of these songs or pieces of music? Make a plan to source one of the pieces of music or songs, and set some time aside to listen to it.

Dare to dance

Many years ago, we were both very moved while watching deaf children dance to music they couldn't 'hear'. They placed their hands on the speakers until they had 'read' the beat and then brought the memory of that music to life on the dance floor. How touchingly similar that scene is to the one of Beethoven laying his head on the piano to 'feel' the music he could no longer hear. Very often, we restrict ourselves and are so self-conscious that we don't give our bodies permission to move and respond spontaneously. When we allow our bodies to really receive and respond to music, it can help us connect with and reignite our inner vitality and passion for life.

Can you dare to allow yourself to dance? Select a piece of music that energises you and makes you feel more alive in yourself when you hear it. Pick a time and a place when you won't be disturbed to allow you to do the following exercise.

Wear loose, comfortable clothing and remove your shoes. Begin to play the music and, as you listen to it, become aware of your body as you stand and of your connection to the ground. Gradually begin to sway gently to the music, moving from side to side until your body's natural rhythm and response to the music takes over. Bring your attention to your arms and gradually allow them to move out and respond to the rhythm of the music in whatever way they choose. Gradually allow your whole body to respond in whatever way it chooses – your head may want to move, your hips might want to become involved. Suspend your inner critic and allow yourself to dare to dance. Have some fun with it!

When you have finished, make a note of any feelings you have and what it was like to experience the spontaneous movement of your body.

_____

_____

_____

_____

Freeing your voice

A Chinese wise man once said, 'When words fail, we sing.' A million love songs witness the triumph of what can be sung over what can be spoken. Maybe you believe you can't sing, and that's okay. We can't all sing, but we can all hum or whistle.

Can you allow your voice to respond, without inhibiting it, to your favourite pieces of music? Repeat the exercise above where you danced to a piece of music, but this time allow your voice to join in, either singing, humming or whistling. Start quietly and gradually, and allow your volume to increase as you become accustomed to your own sound.

Make a note of any feelings you are aware of and how your body feels when you allow your voice to join in the dance.

_____

_____

_____

_____

_____

_____

Reawakening and reintroducing music to your life can help provide an important pathway back to who you are in your deep self and enable you to experience and celebrate the joy of who you are.

Pathway Twenty

Rediscover Nature

He spoke plainly about his bouts of depression, about how the light would leach from the world and the day would grey. Taste and smell were the first senses to go. His ears grew deaf to all but the voices that called him to come deeper down. Touch was the last deserter. Without touch, no texture could excite his soul. 'I hoped,' he said. 'Like a drowning man, I clung to hope when high waves threatened to pull me down; down to where I'd lose all light, where night is day and day is night.'

'But you came back,' I said.

He smiled slowly. 'I walked the dog this morning in the wood. The leaves were fever-red, a stone slept, eiderdowned with moss and, in the grass, a spider had caught diamonds in its web …

One of the ways to help restore hope and foster a deeper connection with your own vitality is to allow yourself to be open to reawakening your connection with nature. The poet William Wordsworth, in his poem 'There Was a Boy', captured the magical quality of this connection. The boy, in the poem, goes at evening to the edges of the hills and he cups his hands to his mouth to mimic the hootings of the owls. The owls return his calls 'with quivering peals and long halloos and screams, and echoes loud, redoubled and redoubled ...' But, sometimes, the owls fall silent and in the silence the boy's heart opens and becomes one with the beauty that surrounds him.

I remember one sultry summer's evening a few years ago, sitting on the bank of a small river as dusk approached. I was lost in my thoughts, almost oblivious to the life around me, gazing at but not really seeing the water flowing by. Suddenly, my trance was disturbed by a very distinctive call coming from the river. I looked up and in an instant was utterly enthralled by the sight of a kingfisher flying past me just above the water line. The majestic flash of colour left me speechless and filled my heart with a great sense of joy and wonder. In that moment, I felt fully alive and connected to all living things. One life, one breath. On dreary winter days when everything seems grey and bleak, I often return to that moment in time when our life paths crossed and am always warmed by the memory.

Do you remember any time in your life when you glimpsed the beauty of life through an encounter with nature? Take a moment in the space below to recall the experience, where you were, how old you were at the time, who was with you and what the feeling was like for you.

_____

_____

_____

_____

_____

_____

Seasons

We too are creatures of nature and nature holds a mirror to the seasons and rhythms of our lives. We are born, nurtured, develop, blossom, harvest, gather, grow old and die. In each season of the heart, the potential for joy, healing and growth is present in nature, waiting to be discovered.

Which is your favourite season? Take a moment to describe the particular qualities of this season to which you are drawn.

_____

_____

_____

_____

Do the qualities you have identified describe in any way aspects of who you are deep within yourself?

_____

_____

_____

_____

Are there ways in which you could begin to express more of these qualities in terms of how you live your life?

_____

_____

_____

_____

Who are you across the seasons of your life?

In this reflective practice, we will work with the images, colours and sounds of the seasons as a metaphor for your own inner journey as you engage with new ways of expressing and experiencing who you are in your life.

Spring

The earth is taut with anticipation,
Grass stubbles on the garden's face.
The tree's bare limbs
Goose-bump with tight buds.
Behind a fan of shrubs
A crocus blushes purple in the shade.
One single, purple crocus, petals furled
To trumpet Hope's arrival to the world.

Spring is a time of new growth and endless possibilities. The tiniest shoots emerge on bare branches hardly visible to the eye. Buds that have been hibernating and nourishing themselves throughout the long winter begin to pop up and stretch out into the light. Birds busily build their nests, preparing for new life.

Close your eyes and imagine some of your favourite images, sounds and colours of spring. Breathe into these images and savour them for a few moments before opening your eyes.

Now ask yourself the following questions:

What is it within you that has been dormant and is longing to emerge?

_____

_____

_____

_____

_____

_____

Where in your life are you experiencing signs of new growth and possibilities?

_____

_____

_____

_____

_____

_____

What are the ways in which you can support and nurture these new signs of growth and possibility?

_____

———————————————————

———————————————————

———————————————————

———————————————————

———————————————————

Summer

Summer is a time of sunshine, warmth and abundance.

Do you remember,
Summer, sieving through the curtains
Summoning from sleep
And breakfast taken standing
One foot tap-tapping,
And bikes, free-wheeling, shrill screaming
Bumping to the beach.
And stepping high, just one step shy
Of cold, shin-slapping tides
Taste of sea salt, smell of seaweed
The painful tip-toe dancing over stones.
The warm embrace of towels
And sandwiches that really were!
And all things tasting sweeter out of doors.
And lying prone in uncombed meadows
Drowning in the deep and deeper blue
Clutching the earth, afraid of falling up.
Enchanting wrists and feet
With chains of daisies

> *While drunken bees headbutted buttercups*
> *All melting in the midday sun.*

Summer is a time when nature dazzles us with its magnificent displays of colour and beauty. Everywhere flowers compete for our attention. Sweet smells fill the air and the world seems fully alive and vibrant. The days are long and carefree and time seems endless.

Close your eyes and imagine some of your favourite images, sounds and colours of summer. Breathe into these images and savour them for a few moments before opening your eyes.

Now ask yourself the following questions:

What are the ways in which you can allow yourself to be seen and heard more in your life?

_____

_____

_____

_____

_____

_____

_____

How can you express more of the vitality and vibrancy of summer in your life?

_____

_____

_____

_____

_____

_____

What supports do you need to allow yourself to fully express who you are?

_____

_____

_____

_____

_____

_____

Autumn

Autumn is a time of warm colours and soft glows. It is a time of ripening and of letting go.

> *Barns glow with new-mown hay,*
> *Apples roost and all the fruits of summer*
> *Sway from rafters, sleep in jars.*
> *This is Earth's storehouse,*
> *All that has budded, blossomed, bore*
> *Is gathered in.*

While fire flames to keep sharp frost at bay
This store will warm us through the darkest day.
Till snows melt, birds sing
And frost-bound winter
Sparkles into spring.

In the wisdom of autumn time, we harvest the fruits of summer that will carry us through the long winter ahead and we let go of what we no longer need. The leaves on the trees do not exit quietly, they depart with a triumphant blaze of colour and glory. It is a time of celebration, preparation and gathering.

Close your eyes and imagine some of your favourite images, sounds and colours of autumn. Breathe into these images and savour them for a few moments before opening your eyes.

Now ask yourself the following questions:

What within you has ripened and is ready for harvesting?

_____

_____

_____

_____

_____

_____

_____

What are you carrying that you no longer need? What do you need to let go of?

_____

_____

_____

_____

_____

How can you express more of the colour and wisdom of autumn in your life?

_____

_____

_____

_____

_____

_____

What do you need to celebrate in your life?

_____

_____

_____

_____

_____

_____

Winter

Winter erases
Each dawn, a tree stands starker
Black limbs against a sombre sky
Charcoal is winter's colour.

Winter caresses
Each furrowed field lies softer
Old weals allayed by winter's balm
Soft snow is winter's blessing.

Winter silences
Nothing to waylay the eye
Blind, the heart turns inward, questing
Reflection is winter's gifting.

Winter composes
The heart is dormant
No birds sing
While heart and bird
Compose anew for spring.

Winter is a time of stillness, of crisp, frosty mornings and foggy breath. Children jump on shiny puddles, shattering ice. Squirrels conserve their energy and curl up warm against the winds. We snuggle up, forever drawn to the fire's glow. It is fireside time – time for stories or long, companionable silences. We take stock of the seasons gone before and anticipate the seasons yet to come. Deep below the earth, unseen, new life is being nourished and protected, waiting for its time to come. Within the home, the leaven of our lives is kneaded in stillness.

Close your eyes and imagine some of your favourite images, sounds and colours of winter. Breathe into these images and savour them for a few moments before opening your eyes.

Now ask yourself the following questions:

What within you needs to slow down and conserve energy? What needs to be protected?

_____

_____

_____

_____

_____

_____

How can you experience more warmth and comfort in your life?

_____

_____

_____

_____

_____

_____

What within you, deep down, is being nourished, waiting for its spring
to come before it takes its tentative steps into the light?

_____

_____

_____

_____

_____

_____

Savouring the moments

In the busyness of the everyday, our senses can become blunted when
we reduce them to their most basic functions. *Doing* distracts us from
being, and from all the possibilities that being can hold. Engaging with
nature is about being present in a different way to the life and beauty
that surrounds us. Savouring is what enables us to do this. It enables
the outside world come in and impress itself on our hearts.

I grew up with city-dwellers who saw and savoured roof slates
steaming a soft incense after rain. They were people who listened
to and savoured a hailstorm play a drum sequence on their dustbins,

people who caressed and savoured the texture of old stone buildings as they went about the business of their day.

Sometimes savouring the little things makes it possible to bear the big things. It's almost as if we need to suck the marrow of what is good and beautiful to endure and survive hardship and evil. Viktor Frankl, an Austrian neurologist and psychiatrist, was imprisoned in a concentration camp by the Nazis in 1944 but survived the Holocaust. His subsequent book – *Man's Search for Meaning*[12] – teaches us that it is possible, even in the midst of enormous deprivation and suffering, to savour the beauty of a sunset.

As the inner life of the prisoner tended to become more intense, he also experienced the beauty of art and nature as never before. Under their influence he sometimes even forgot his own frightful circumstances. If someone had seen our faces on the journey from Auschwitz to a Bavarian camp as we beheld the mountains of Salzburg with their summits glowing in the sunset, through the little barred windows of the prison carriage, he would never have believed that those were the faces of men who had given up all hope of life and liberty. Despite that factor – or maybe because of it – we were carried away by nature's beauty, which we had missed for so long.

In camp too, a man might draw the attention of a comrade working next to him to a nice view of the setting sun shining through the tall trees of the Bavarian woods (as in the famous watercolour by Dürer), the same woods in which we had built an enormous, hidden munitions plant. One evening, when we were already resting on the floor of our hut, dead tired, soup bowls in hand, a fellow prisoner rushed in and asked us to run out to the assembly grounds and see the wonderful sunset. Standing outside we saw sinister clouds glowing in the west and the whole sky alive with clouds of ever-changing shapes and colors, from steel blue to blood red. The desolate grey mud huts provided a sharp contrast, while the puddles on the muddy ground reflected the glowing sky. Then, after minutes of moving silence, one prisoner said to another, 'How beautiful the world could be!'

Wherever you are, you are a human spirit and even in the most extreme and unlikely circumstances, your spirit is capable of savouring.

Savouring an experience winnows the wheat of joy from the chaff of the humdrum. When we savour the small miracles, we season the everyday.

When we model savouring, we flavour the imaginations, senses and spirits of our own children.

My father and grandfather were city men who had a passion for the countryside. Every weekend, we were taken for a walk to a cow-dung-scented small road that skirted a valley – I would have preferred to hunch with a book before the fire. I remember their enthusiasm for stone walls and buttered gorse. The small stream that lazed through the valley was to them a thing of beauty; the blue mountains in the distance a mystery. My brother and I ran hither and yon, chivvying the men to walk faster. We were to learn that slow walking leads to deeper seeing, smelling, feeling and tasting.

I remember the smells of bluebells and the velvet texture of primroses. High grass in the meadows tickled our shins and soaked our socks and there was the gritty cold of the water from the roadside well to fortify us for the trek home. Day by day, year by year, the mysteries of the countryside worked their magic on the city boys.

Now, I live in a valley. A river drains the valley floor and trees inhabit the slopes above the flood meadows. I have learned to amble; to walk slowly and savour the sights and smells. I meet people who walk briskly. 'Good for the heart,' they say as they pound by. I suspect the heart is also nourished by lichen beards on branches or a heron, high-stepping in the shallows or the purl of the water as it weaves around a granite stone dropped by some long-gone glacier.

It helps to have an old dog, a younger Labrador and at least one son in tow. The younger ones leap ahead from one adventure to the next. I take the old dog's pace and see mica glinting in small stones; the two-toed prints of shy deer, the whorl of flattened grass where they passed the night. I hear the trees sieve the wind, the sharp call of a hunting hawk, the whirr of a startled duck. I smell the green of ferns and the resin sweating from still trees. Sometimes, the old dog just throws herself down in the grass and lolls her tongue to savour the air. I sit down beside her, fill my pipe and enjoy the moment.

Some years ago, I took one of my boys down to fish the river. At the time, I still thought fishing was about catching fish but the slow murmur of the river lulled me into a deep awareness of the beauty that surrounded us. Suddenly, a kingfisher hovered over the water. I like to think it was the same kingfisher that Linda encountered. Its wings were a blur as it batted the air, its plumage was iridescent, as if someone had dipped the little bird in oil. 'Look!' I said, and before our boy could lift his eyes from the river, the kingfisher had flitted away.

'What was it?' he asked.

'A kingfisher,' I said.

Some years later, we were reading in companionable silence. 'What does "enchanted" mean?' he asked.

'It means to be captivated,' I answered, 'to see something so wonderful that, for a moment, the rest of the world ceases to exist.'

'You were enchanted the day you saw the kingfisher,' he smiled as he returned to his book.

The pathways of our senses

The different senses we have – sight, sound, smell, touch and taste – each provide unique pathways that enable us to really experience and savour the fullness and richness of life. However, when we are stressed or down or just very busy we tend, without even being aware of it, to engage with the world in a limited and restricted way, living mostly out of our dominant sense. We become aware of our other senses only when we are jolted by nasty intrusions that are outside of our control, such as a loud bang or a foul smell.

What is your dominant sense? The sense that you depend on the most? Even though your other senses are often not consciously in your awareness, their pathways are always there and can help you to have a richer and deeper engagement with the world around you. It's a bit like the excitement of having a 3D or high-definition experience.

In the remainder of this chapter, we will explore ways to help you receive the fullness of what your other senses have to offer you.

Take a moment to consider in turn each of your senses.

Smell

My favourite smells always fill me with a sense of joy and excitement. I love the salty smell of the sea or the smell of a cow's hot breath in the air on a crisp, frosty morning. I also love the smell of newly cut grass or the smell of freshly baked bread.

Call to mind some of your favourite smells and name any feeling or particular memories that you associate with these smells.

_____

_____

_____

_____

Ask yourself what it would be like for you if you could increase your contact with some of your favourite smells.

_____

_____

_____

_____

What steps could you take in the next week to increase this contact?

_____

_____

_____

_____

Taste

Experience what it is like to taste flavours one at a time. How do you taste – do you leave enough time to savour a taste before you swallow?

What are your favourite tastes? I love the taste of raspberries and fresh pineapple. Do you prefer sweet or savoury tastes? Hot or cold? What tastes do you like to mix?

Call to mind some of your favourite tastes and name any feeling or particular memories you associate with these tastes.

_____

_____

_____

_____

Ask yourself what it would be like for you if you could slow down and really savour what you taste.

_____

_____

_____

_____

What steps could you take to help you to do this?

_____

_____

_____

_____

Touch

Our sense of touch is one of the most powerful bridges we have to a deep contact with others and with ourselves. Just as the Inuit have many words to describe snow, we have many ways to describe touch – gentle, warm, tender, loving, friendly, secure, playful. The caress of a lover. The strong embrace of a friend. The feel of rain on my neck. The soft touch of a baby's skin. A warm handshake. When we are parting, we invite people to stay in touch, stay connected.

What positive memories or associations do you have connected with your sense of touch?

_____

_____

_____

_____

Ask yourself what it would be like for you if you could engage your sense of touch more in your contact with others.

_____

_____

_____

_____

What steps could you take to help you to do this? What are the ways in which you hold yourself back when it comes to expressing yourself through touch?

_____

_____

_____

_____

Hearing

Our sense of hearing is our gateway to a thriving, boisterous, musical universe. The sounds we listen to can move us to tears or fill us with joy. I love the soulful sound of the cello, the sound of rain on a metal roof, the sound of the wind on a stormy night, the sound of my favourite singer, the sound of my sons laughing.

What sounds do you love?

Describe your favourite sounds and any positive memories or associations you have with your sense of hearing. What sounds do you find most nourishing?

_____

_____

_____

_____

Ask yourself what it would be like for you if you could make more room in your life for these favourite sounds.

_____

_____

_____

_____

What would it be like to really listen deeply to yourself?

_____

_____

_____

_____

What steps could you take to help you to engage more with your sense of hearing? What within you needs to be heard?

_____

_____

_____

_____

Sight

I welcome the shy blush of dawn that stencils hills from the lightening sky, bringing form and colour to the waking world. As that world turns, I watch the light flow into clefts and folds, revealing and concealing the everyday wonders of my world. So many sights, yet none sweeter to the heart than the faces of loved ones enlivened by the light.

What are your favourite sights? Describe any feelings or memories you associate with these sights.

_____

_____

_____

_____

*What would it be like for you if you could become more aware of the
beautiful sights all around you ?*

_____

_____

_____

*Ask yourself what it would be like if you could slow down and savour
the world as you experience it through your sense of sight. If you could
allow yourself to look deeply at what you see?*

_____

_____

_____

Sensory walk, a reflective practice – twenty to thirty minutes

When we engage fully with all our senses, we can experience a different
quality of presence to ourselves and the world around us. A quality of
presence that can be deeply nourishing and healing. This is particularly
true when we are fully in contact with nature. As part of this reflective
practice exercise, you are invited to choose a place to walk where you
will be surrounded by nature. It could be your local park, the banks
of a canal, somewhere by the sea or a woodland. Put twenty to thirty
minutes aside to do this walk at a time when you won't feel hurried or
feel under pressure to be somewhere else.

Before beginning your walk, breathe in deeply for a count of three and breathe out for a count of five. Repeat this breathing pattern three times before starting to walk. As you begin your walk, bring your awareness to the fact that you are walking through a living, throbbing universe that is fully alive and vital. Remind yourself of your openness to feeling the pulsation of that universe and to being curious about it.

While walking, try to remain fully present to yourself. Be aware of the connection between your legs and feet and the ground. Be mindful of how you are walking. Try to walk tall in the full height of yourself. Imagine there is a string going from the top of your head to the clouds above. Let your arms hang loosely by your side.

As you walk, bring your awareness to the following senses individually.

1. Become aware of the sights around you.
   The sights of other walkers, animals, insects or birds. Be aware of what you can see close to you and what is far away. Look from side to side as you walk. Notice the colours, the shape and structure of the trees or grasses. Notice their height and form. Notice any movement in the water. Pause for a moment and look up to the sky. Bring your awareness to the clouds. Watch the pattern of their movement. Notice any birds flying, watch the rhythm of their flight. Look down from time to time and notice the shape and contours of the ground you are on. Seeing and walking with awareness.

2. **Bring your attention now to your sense of hearing.**

The sound of your feet as they make contact with the ground. The sound of other walkers. The sound of nearby animals or insects. Bees buzzing. Birds singing. The sound of the wind. Faraway sounds. Sounds that are very faint and hardly there, sounds that make themselves heard. Be aware of the sounds that you are most drawn to. The sounds you want to hear more of. Walking and hearing with awareness.

3. **As you walk, bring your awareness to your sense of touch.**

Notice the touch of your clothes against your skin. Notice the breeze as it touches your face. As you walk, allow yourself to stop and touch different shapes and textures that you are drawn to. Feel the strong bark of a tree, the soft touch of moss on a stone. Become aware of the sensation of making contact with water. The rain falling on your palm. The feel of different leaves and grasses. The smooth touch of a pebble. The texture of a leaf. Walking and feeling with awareness.

4. **Bring your awareness to your sense of smell.**

Breathe in deeply through your nose. Notice the different scents floating on the breeze.

The smell of nearby cows in a field. The fragrance of flowers as you pass. The smell of the sea. The smell of freshly cut grass. The dank smell of the earth. The smell of a fire burning in the distance. Smells that are pleasant, smells that are unpleasant. Walking with a deeper awareness of your sense of smell.

5. Now try to complete the rest of the walk while engaging all your senses.

   Don't try to force it – just maintain an attentive presence to all of your senses and experience yourself and the world around you in this way. Be aware of anything that surprises you.

   Note what draws your attention in your journal. Walking with an awareness of all your senses.

   Later, when you have completed your walk, take a few moments to write in your journal about what the experience was like for you.

Endnotes

1. Carr, A. (2011). *Positive Psychology: The Science of Happiness and Human Strengths* (Second Edition). London:Routledge
2. Hamlet, II. ii 1350-1351
3. Beck, A.T. (1976). *Cognitive Therapy and the Emotional Disorders*. New York: International University Press
    Ellis, A. (1994). *Reason and Emotion in Psychotherapy*. New York: Citadel Press
    Burns, D. (1980). *Feeling Good: The New Mood Therapy*. New York: Penguin Books
4. Greenberger, D., Padesky, C.A. (1995). *Mind Over Mood*. New York: The Guilford Press
5. Greenberger, D., Padesky, C.A. (1995). *Mind Over Mood*. New York: The Guilford Press
6. Bourne, E.J. (1990). *The Anxiety and Phobia Handbook*. Oakland, CA: New Harbinger Publications
7. Excerpt from 'The Joseph Coat' by Christy Kenneally. (Originally published by Gilbert Dalton, 1997). For full text of poem see Appendix A.
8. Excerpt from 'Dear Parents' by Christy Kenneally. For full text of poem see Appendix B.
9. Excerpt from 'The Joseph Coat' by Christy Kenneally. (Originally published by Gilbert Dalton, 1997). For full text of poem see Appendix A.
10. Carr, A. (2011). *Positive Psychology: The Science of Happiness and Human Strengths* (Second Edition). London: Routledge
11. Excerpt from 'The Joseph Coat' by Christy Kenneally. (Originally published by Gilbert Dalton, 1997). For full text of poem see Appendix A.
12. Frankl, Viktor E. (1959). *Man's Search for Meaning*. New York: Pocket Books

Appendix A

Joseph's coat was the coat of many colours given to the Old Testament character by his father as a sign of his favour. I was a child of my time and my people and I wrote 'The Joseph Coat 'as a tribute to the people who wove colours of belonging into my heart and favoured me with their love'.

The Joseph Coat

I write of those
who wove my Joseph Coat
and left their imprimatur
on that part of me
I call a soul.
It is not
that I have fallen out of love
but, what was passion absence has distilled
And many pages
of my father's shilling-jotter
have woven a tapestry

of living fibres
for the boy
who'd grown away.
Now, in his modern mind
it hangs;
the final Temple veil
before his self.

Lizzie's mother closed her eyes
and saw such sights
as she had never dreamed
for the century that she had lived.
She left her daughter
dowried with the candy-shop,
a picture full of posing, patriot dead,
a sharp tongue,
deft fingers,
few friendship and a rocking chair.
Murph and I were acolytes
at the polished shrine
and brought the votive,
Evening Echo offering
to confirm what she already knew,
that we might, also,
on the strength of that good deed,
take turns
to cowboy-ride her rocking chair.
And, while I rocked,
she crochet-talked
of days gone by
and wove fine, coloured threads

across the sepia picture memory
of my mother.
In satchel-strap
and school-cap, happy days,
a flood of runny noses
boiled around her shop
to but a sticky ha'porth
chisel-chipped from the glacier
on a black slab
in the curtained kitchen.

She died, with neither chick nor child
to throw the clay.
Fickle flowers,
fast grown restless
mitch from grave to grave
and ring-a-rosy round
with every playful wind.
A son, would write her epitaph
on stone or with a pen
as I do now,
for she had none.
'Manuscript face,
etched with lettering of age
rocking, in the chair-beat of my heart
silent.
Wordless coming
Wordless going
home to the womb of clay
earth-song sung.
Withered

wordless
living Amen
fragile
spirit-holding vessel
child-dreams lull thee.'

When God made Sam
He hadn't much to spare
and made him small
and hunched his back
to keep him ever like a child
and love him more
than people who grew straight.
Or, so his mother said
and spoke a truth
concealed from learned men.
And God,
to balance off His selfish act
had placed within
this crooked, oyster of a manchester pearl;
a singing voice
to purr out healthy notes
and shush the rosary of sparrows
on the roof.

At Christmas time
when pillow-slipped puddings
swung from fresh-washed banisters,
and rubber bands
held little, plastic Jesus in his crib,
he'd doff his cap and reverently swear

that Arthur Guinness was his patron saint
to watch the fairy-lights of indignation
rosy-red his sister's cheeks
and warm the cockles of his heart
on her furnace-blast description
of the fires of Hell.

His brother Con, had asked
if I would bring him Christ on Christmas day,
then kissed my hands,
for he had neither frankincense nor myrrh
to show his thanks.
I went with Michael, once,
to chat
and wrote these lines
to show my love.

'No beer, fag, cup in the hand,
they have shag-all.'
So, script prepared
we double-breasted, Sunday-stepped
to the plain, brown door
and pushed into the bedroom where he lay.
As always, napkined with a fresh Examiner.
sipping the bottomless cup of tea.
He had been a carpenter, once
Chiselling, planing, varnishing,
with a proud eye
sturdy struts and solid door-jambs,
stools too and cots for other's children,
it being 'the will of God'.

And, when the same will struck him in his prime
sickness spiralled slowly, lower, closer,
and twisted tree-roots of his tradesman's fingers
as if the ravaged grain of oak and ash
bled vengeful sap into his bones
and gnarled therein, their former shapes.
Had we been younger,
he had given us sweets
and savoured our pleasure.
As it was, he gifted our stories
with a laugh; precious and painful.
Our parting was wordless;
pain forbade fingers to deputise
and so, he wished us well and happy.
And we went up out of that place
grateful for the sun's warmth
and our footsteps,
sounding in the silent lane.

'I married twice,
had six to rear.
What, love?
God help your head.'
In one short breath
could Betty quote her life.
All her chicks, save one,
had feathered, fought and flown
to have their own
and phone her from abroad
on Christmas Day.
'I'm grand,' she'd shout

to bridge the gap.
'I'd love to come, Mam.'
'Save your money, boy,' she'd roar
and trumpet-blow her nose
to clear her eyes.
And with her many stories of 'long 'go'
she aired the blind-drawn places in my heart
where mother should have been
and spoke of her with laughs
and sometimes tears,
that I began to feel
like someone's child;
Maura's boy -
and not so much alone ...

'He did a hobble,' someone said
but none could say for sure
except that he had closed his door
to live, a recluse in his way;
a drop-out coral-seed
in the reef of life.
Three generations of children
flowed and ebbed before his dry-docked door
and Dermot stayed within
a monument
to things that might have been.

Hughie's mother
risked him out to play
at nine,
for the first time.

And when, all in a day,
he belly-busted
in an April-shower lake
and dripped the gleaming lino
of her Brasso'd mausoleum,
it was too late for second thoughts;
for, he had piloted his match-stick brig
and scaled the Convent wall
risking excommunication, broken glass, barbed wire
and all
and, having seen the sun from such a height
would never linger further in her shade.
And when his cycle skidded on the road,
she hardly knew what words to say
or how to weep,
her son had been so long away.

I lastly took my pen
to write the praises
of a man I loved
above all others,
save my father,
and never wrote a single word.
I laid my pen aside,
happy that years and miles
had not yet dimmed that passion
to memory.

Appendix B

I was deeply moved by the men and women of A Little Lifetime Foundation who grieve their precious babies who died before or shortly after birth. So many of those parents had been told they'd 'get over it' or they'd 'have another', as if their baby could be forgotten or replaced.

I wrote this poem to affirm the love they have for the babies who had lived their full span of life 'within your body and within your love'. I was deeply honoured when my poem was carved on the monument in Glasnevin cemetery that marks and honours the final resting place of over 50,000 babies.

Dear Parents
I did not die young.
I lived my span of life
within your body and within your love.
There are many, who have lived long lives
and not been loved as me.
If you would honour me
then, speak my name
and number me among your family.

If you would honour me
then live in love
for, in that love, I live.
Never doubt that we will meet again.
Until that happy day,
I will grow with God
and wait for you.